HOW
TO
FISH

Casting at the Sun
The Deepening Pool
The Secret Carp
A Passion for Angling
Four Seasons
River Diary
Falling in Again

HOW
TO
FISH

CHRIS
YATES

HAMISH HAMILTON
London

HAMISH HAMILTON

Published by the Penguin Group
Penguin Books Ltd, 80 Strand, London WC2R 0RL, England
Penguin Group (USA) Inc., 375 Hudson Street, New York, New York 10014, USA
Penguin Group (Canada), 90 Eglinton Avenue East, Suite 700, Toronto, Ontario, Canada M4P 2Y3
(a division of Pearson Penguin Canada Inc.)
Penguin Ireland, 25 St Stephen's Green, Dublin 2, Ireland (a division of Penguin Books Ltd)
Penguin Group (Australia), 250 Camberwell Road, Camberwell, Victoria 3124, Australia
(a division of Pearson Australia Group Pty Ltd)
Penguin Books India Pvt Ltd, 11 Community Centre, Panchsheel Park, New Delhi – 110 017, India
Penguin Group (NZ), cnr Airborne and Rosedale Roads, Albany, Auckland 1310, New Zealand
(a division of Pearson New Zealand Ltd)
Penguin Books (South Africa) (Pty) Ltd, 24 Sturdee Avenue, Rosebank, Johannesburg 2196, South Africa

Penguin Books Ltd, Registered Offices: 80 Strand, London WC2R 0RL, England

www.penguin.com

First published 2006
1

Copyright © Christopher Yates, 2006

The moral right of the author has been asserted

Set in 12/16.5 pt Monotype Dante
Typeset by Rowland Phototypesetting Ltd, Bury St Edmunds, Suffolk
Printed in Great Britain by Clays Ltd, St Ives plc

A CIP catalogue record for this book is available from the British Library

ISBN-13: 978-0-241-14330-8
ISBN-10: 0-241-14330-6

To Camilla, Alex, Will and Ellen, my patient children;
and also to Jason, who showed me the river.

With my silken line and delicate hook
I wander into a myriad of ripples
And find – freedom.

Li Yu, *Fisherman's Song*

CONTENTS

CONTENTS

Acknowledgements

A smudged collection of bankside jottings would never have metamorphosed into this final form had it not been for the regular promptings of Dan Kieran, Tom Hodgkinson and Kevin Parr, editors and correspondent to the *Idler* magazine. My grateful thanks to them, and also to my youngest daughter, Ellen, who typed up the manuscript – sometimes faster than I could dictate it!

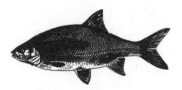

FIRST
CAST

*The
River
Speaks in
Ripples*

However eager I am to start fishing there is something about the first glimpse of a river that never fails to stop me in my tracks. Even on a wet winter's morning when I'm hurrying with all my gear across an open field a river will flag me down before I can find a sheltering tree and for a few moments we have a silent conversation.

First I must have the news, although, with a river, it's mostly old news: how the water has risen or coloured since the storm of four days ago; how the weed along a chosen pool has almost disappeared since a gang of swans mowed through it last week;

how the flow has lost its energy after a month of clear skies. Obviously this kind of information is important, especially if it feeds my optimism rather than makes me wish I'd stayed in bed, but the factual stuff is dealt with in seconds; I must wait a minute longer for whatever else the river has to say.

I am looking at the water now, but it was a morning ago and at a different place that I had my first glimpse of it. I was standing in a sloping field overlooking this small lowland stream as it meandered between high banks overgrown with willow, sedge and alder. I could see that the level was low for the time of year and therefore knew the current would be correspondingly slow and the water probably crystal clear. There was an early morning breeze breaking up the reflections of the trees. A few fallen leaves were floating downstream, but no fishes rippled the surface, nor was there any sparkle in it as the September sun had yet to appear above the hills to the east. As I looked down on the sweeping bend below me something in my memory or my bones made me instantly decide that I should head upstream rather than down towards the more familiar water where I'd intended to go. I had never explored the upper reaches of this particular stretch before, but it seemed that today I would be casting into new pools.

The slow breeze swam along with the slow current, making smooth ripples that said it was easier to follow the flow than go against it, especially first thing in the morning when everything must be effortless. Yet below the ripples there was this contradictory voice, a countercurrent, working like divination, but probably triggered by something less mysterious. I think the morning's weather and the morning's light had combined with the river to release the flow of all the countless other rivers I'd ever fished. One momentary glance and there was an unconscious welling up of historic waters, superimposing themselves one after the other on the present scene until there must have been an almost perfect match because why else was I suddenly trying to remember a different river that ran through a day similar to this one, but maybe ten, twenty or even thirty years ago?

Happy to be acting on a whim – or a seeming whim – I turned left and began walking upstream, keeping my eyes on the water as much as I could, although there were occasional willow thickets, hedges and ditches where I lost sight of it and had to turn aside to find a new path. Even where the banks were reasonably clear it was still sometimes difficult to see much of the river. Despite the first witherings of autumn there are sections where bulrush and lily beds remain like bristling forests and gently swaying swamps stretching from bank to bank. In the quieter glides and shallower runs, long streamers of ribbon weed are all yellowing at their tips, making them appear semi-transparent as they weave in the current, but they still obscure much of the actual riverbed and, as I watchfully made my way upstream, they were also concealing what I was looking for.

September: one of the loveliest and most generous months in the angler's calendar. Even if the weather doesn't change much after a hot, dry and miserly August, the lengthening nights, the heavy dews, the cooler mornings and evenings remind the fish that the summer is almost over and they must therefore grab what they can before winter comes. In a few weeks time, after the equinox and the first serious weather of the year, the river will be transformed from a chain of quiet, secretive pools into a deeper, stronger and continuous flow. All the midstream vegetation will be swept away and the fish will have to change their habits and their haunts.

Changing habits and haunts at the end of summer was something I did all through my formative years, just like everyone else, so maybe my urge to explore new territory today was prompted less by a vague memory of another river and more by a conditioned reflex. Sixteen slightly intimidating Septembers, each one confronting me with new classrooms, new tutors, new books and new problems, must have left their mark. Alternatively, I'm seeking new water because of a genetic memory, an echo from those millennia when, every autumn, my ancestors followed the migrating herds southwards.

Heading upstream, I naturally had more chance of spotting fish as I was approaching them from behind; however, the rising sun threw a long shadow ahead of me and, at a turn in the river, it must have been cast across a group of chub because there was a sudden plunging splash. Until that moment, all I'd seen since I'd arrived were shoals of minnows flickering through the few weed-free, shallower glides and it was reassuring to be startled by such a walloping commotion. They must have been quite large fish – it looked and sounded as if someone had just heaved in a sack of potatoes – but I'm convinced they were chub. Several bow waves shot off in different directions, some of them sweeping into the reed bed on the far bank, which is typical of chub if they're spooked. I crept up to where the ripples were subsiding and waited a few minutes to see if anything was going to reappear.

Years ago, when I was a chub devotee, I would have waited all day just for a glimpse of one of those creatures, but today I'm not really interested in them: I have another more resplendent fish on my mind.

Fifty yards after the chub hole, I came to a seductive willow-shrouded pool which seemed to possess all the features I'd been looking for: a shelving riverbed where a steady current slowed and divided around the remains of a sunken tree, the main flow deflected over to the far bank, the rest coming round in a slow idling whirl beneath the overhanging willows. There were some frayed late-season lilies and a thin weed bed, but the shade had obviously suppressed their summer growth and, apart from the timber reef, the pool was reasonably free of obstructions. Despite the clarity of the water, the depth, the shade and the reflections made it almost impossible to see if any fish were at home, so I set up my rod and reel, tied on a hook, baited with a worm and cast out.

However impatient I am to get to the river, if I'm not completely familiar with it and it refuses to make any promises, hours can pass before I finally decide where to make my first cast. But once I've chosen the place it's a matter of life and death that I cast immediately. When I get the feeling that *this is the spot*, there's no fiddling about with fancy rigs or sophisticated presentations. I might sometimes muster just enough restraint to allow a float or a weight to be attached to the line, but if anything takes longer than about thirty seconds to set up I feel as if a prison door is closing on me. All my expectations, frustrations, all the pretence about being happy doing other things in the days while I wasn't fishing – everything is resolved as soon as the line is in the water and I'm reconnected with reality.

My bait slowly sank into the depths of midstream

and I checked its descent by gently tensioning the line so that the worm would come round into the underbank eddy where I thought the fish might be waiting. First cast into an undiscovered, unknown pool; anything could be down there; anything could happen. The line twitched, began to tighten, fell slack, twitched, fell slack once more. Minnows? Chublets? Even before the line moved I sensed the river might've deceived me with this perfect-looking place; it was perhaps too obviously a lair or a sanctuary for a big fish. Later in the season when the heavier currents made any deep backflow more appealing, it would almost certainly hold something rod-splitting, but to-day the river's generally slow pace made it suddenly seem, contrary to my first impression, just too sopor-ific. Finally the line made a steady decisive movement and I upped sharply with the rod tip – and reeled in a bare hook.

Almost certainly a minnow, I thought, or, more likely, a dozen minnows all fighting over one worm. I re-baited and cast again – the second cast less urgent, more leisurely, more considered than the first. Min-nows, I told myself, were a sign of a healthy river and despite their worm-whittling presence in my pool, there was still a chance that much bigger fish were lurking nearby. Once more the line began to hesitantly tighten and slacken as soon as the bait sank to the bottom. Then, again, the steadier draw, but this time I connected – and the curving rod tip told me it definitely wasn't a minnow. Something went round deep down in a couple of tight circles, but though my old cane rod remained nicely bent not an inch of line clicked off the reel and I eased the fish towards me. I was sure I recognized the soft thump of the tail stroke and its identity was confirmed when it swirled and skittered on the surface, showing a lovely blue flank. Mixed up in the spray, the bright red fins looked like radiating beams of light. It came over the net without any more fuss; I hoisted it ashore, dampened my hands on the wet mesh, quickly unhooked it, guessed it at a pound and a quarter and slipped it back into its home – the first roach of my season, but an accidental one.

Using such a universally attractive bait as a worm in such a richly diverse habitat as this river is a test of faith. It's easy if I can see the fish I'm after, but in a deep hole or in amongst the reeds there's probably only a one in five chance of connecting with whatever I'm after. Sometimes, especially late in the season, I like to fully embrace the serendipitous nature of the fishing by seeing how many different species I can catch using the same method in a series of randomly chosen swims; yet despite the low water, September is too good a month for such an unselective approach. I may be using a bait that's appetizing to every kind of fish in the river, but I have only one kind of fish swimming in my head. As long as I can keep it bright enough and don't allow it to sink down under a shadow of doubt, it will eventually rise to the surface and, like the lost river, find its perfect match.

SECOND
CAST

*A Seasonal
Obsession*

Having settled into what he considers to be the best-looking swim on the river, an angler will often fish steadfastly all day despite the fact that the river makes it obvious that he's made the wrong choice. Sometimes it's just pride that prevents him searching for a better spot, or laziness or simply the fact that he's got too much equipment to lug about from place to place. I should have moved on as soon as I'd caught the roach. I'm not interested in roach today, but I had to have another few casts because the pool looked so inviting, and I continued to catch roach though all much smaller than the first. Then, after perhaps half an hour, the minnows began to get voracious and I caught several, each of whom engulfed worms longer than themselves. This was the river wagging fish fingers of admonishment at me.

Later on, maybe tomorrow or next week when the level rises and the current begins to zip, the pool will almost certainly harbour something worthwhile, but today it was, apart from one reasonable fish, only fit for tiddlers. I reeled in, retreated and set off again upstream.

The willows and alders gradually gave way to more open ground. There were two or three interesting-looking glides and one dark pool above a reed bed that winked at me in a slightly sinister pike-ish kind of way. Then, for perhaps two hundred yards, I followed a straight featureless bank broken by only a few yellowing elder bushes. The water was sluggish, deep and uninspiring, and however much I told myself that big fish often haunt the most apparently mundane places, I didn't even pause for a closer look being impatient to reach the bend ahead where a gleaming of ripples told me something was happening. Only as I approached did I realize that it wasn't fish who were breaking the surface, but birds. A large flock of swallows was pouring down out of the blue, converging on a large alder which slanted across the inside of the bend. The birds were coming in low around it, skimming the water, breaking up the tree's dark reflection with a speckling of small quick splashes. Were they scooping floating insects or had they all decided this was an ideal spot for a drink and a bath? I watched them for a while and decided definitely the latter. As I walked slowly past them they didn't vacate the area, seeming indifferent to me, caught up in their pre-migration excitement.

The tree was almost horizontal, but perfectly healthy, its roots having re-established a hold on the bank after some previous winter flood had undermined them. I made my way carefully around it, and even before I saw the pool above I felt a little surge of euphoria, knowing that I'd finally arrived at the place I was looking for.

The first thing I spotted when I peered into the clear water was the black tail of a chub working in the current under the far bank. The reflections made it difficult to see the rest of the fish, but it was probably quite a big one, maybe five pounds. A simple flick across the river with a worm and it would have almost certainly been mine. The friend who first introduced me to this stretch catches most of his chub on a dry fly, and had an accidental six-pounder on a mayfly when he was stalking trout. But, as I said, I'm not interested in chub or roach and nor can I be bothered with trout; the fish that swims in my head, eager to compare itself with its authentic counterpart, is a perch.

On this river, from now until the middle of March when the season ends, I'm a perch angler and all my efforts and hopes will be directed towards this one particular species. Occasionally I may veer off to some other stream to fish for barbel or grayling and in summer I prefer to cast into ponds and lakes for carp and tench, but these last few seasons, once autumn arrives, I have become ever more impassioned about perch. A few miles downstream, I've landed some brilliant creatures to over three pounds – and a three-pounder is a big perch by my standards. But Jason, my local informant who knows this stretch of river better than anyone, recently had a monster of over five pounds. Only once in my life have I even dreamt of such a perch, and then, in the dream, it wasn't me who caught it. Yet all perch look impressive and on an otherwise dull winter's day a fish of a pound with its vivid colours, its striking markings and its superbly bristling demeanour, can send an otherwise dull angler into raptures.

Today is my first day here this season. I made an unusually early start (for me) because I thought the recent cool nights might make the perch – who get listless in warm weather – more active in the morning. Also there was an optimistic weather forecast. Last September, on a similar kind of day I found a shoal of biggish fish hanging about quite brazenly in the middle of a quiet pool. They reminded me of a gang of hooligans as they showed off their tribal insignia, raised their superbly intimidating dorsals and launched sudden attacks on the schools of innocent minnows. But there was more water in the river then. Because of the unusually dry winter and spring, the level has been gently falling all season and today I suspect that even the cockiest young perch will be skulking under the cover of overhanging trees or merging his zebra-striped flanks into the swaying verticals of the reed beds.

While they may not be under constant threat from pike, otters and herons, they must feel more vulnerable with their habitat reduced by about a third. More importantly, however, their own feeding habits have been limited for the same reason; everything below them in the food chain is behaving more furtively, or is less attainable because of the increase in unswimmable shallows and compressed impenetrable weed beds. Maybe my chances of a big fish have also been reduced accordingly. But then again, unusual conditions can often lead to unusual opportunities.

The curved pool above the alder is at its deepest along the near bank where decades of winter scouring have tilted the whole riverbed down towards where I'm now fishing. I have concealed myself amongst the old nettles and hogweed and I'm now looking back towards the tree, which lies like an overgrown dam across the pool's tail. I have cast an unweighted worm to drift beneath the trailing branches, but because of the slowness of the current the bait is only being carried under the fringe of them rather than deeply into their shadow, where I'm convinced something is waiting.

Unlike the eager optimism I felt for the first pool, which was based solely on its appearance, and which faded almost as soon as I cast into it, what's interesting here is that I've been fishing for hours without a bite and yet I still feel as certain about its potential as when I first approached it.

A dozen other anglers could scout along these banks and would consider this an ideal spot for perch; however, this river has a hot-seeming perch hole round every other bend but, because of the small number of roving shoals, only a few will actually contain any fish; also the largest specimens, the ones I'm dreaming about, are often solitary, which makes them even harder to find, especially along such a jungly stream. This is, I admit, a delightful-looking pool, but I've fallen in love with it not for its smile, but because of its intensity. It has a kind of indefinable energy about it and if I can forget about the chub and the fact that a pike would like lairing here as much as a perch, I think I could be happy to remain here till next spring – or at least until teatime.

I am not a patient angler, but it can look that way because I am so enthusiastic. For instance, I can sit on an overhanging branch all day if there's a chance of dropping a bait on a big fish passing unsuspecting beneath it. I may only get one chance here – and the reel will screech at me should the moment arrive – but until then, or until I finally reel in, I shall enjoy waiting while watching the river sliding past me and the swallows skimming past the river.

This being my first visit of the season, I'm probably paying more attention to detail than normal if only to reassure myself that everything is as lovely as it was last time (there are only very few places that an angler revisits without an initial almost parental concern). Having settled down against this comfortable bank I'm free now to cast, to lean my rod on a cunningly trimmed stem of hogweed and to scribble down some observations – some sketches – while I'm fishing. However, writing while fishing can prove to be a complete waste of time, especially on a river. Two years ago I was sitting like this, notebook on knee writing a glowing account of a wonderful day's angling that I thought had just ended. But it hadn't ended. I'd casually re-cast the rod and after maybe twenty minutes a fish swept up the bait, dragged the rod tip round and panicked the reel. It was such a violent contact that I jumped up as I reached for the rod, sending the notebook flying into the river. As I tussled with a stubbornly tenacious barbel, the book floated away downstream, its open pages looking like the wings of a drowning bird.

THIRD
CAST

*The
Endless
Stream*

Glancing upstream just then, I saw a small silver dace, maybe six inches long, leap high out of the water. A few moments later, the same fish leapt again. There was no obvious reason for such aquabatics, as it didn't appear to be trying to catch flying insects, nor was it being pursued by a predator. I suppose it may have been trying to shake off some irritating leech or tickling river bug, but then again it might merely have been feeling frisky – like when a shoal of minnows in shallow water is tumbling and somersaulting about in apparent playfulness.

It's never obvious why a fish should suddenly rocket

through the surface, but some species seem to make a habit of it. Carp, for instance, appear to take a special delight in making spectacular, walloping jumps; trout, barbel and, of course, salmon are all regular leapers. Roach and bream often roll on the surface prior to feeding, but I've never seen a perch behave in this way, nor have I encountered one who jumped clear of the water, though I'm certain it must occasionally happen. I've seen perch causing dramatic waves and upswirls, with just a glimpse of a raised dorsal fin cutting the surface as they pursue their prey, but, usually, they like to lurk deep down or in amongst concealing reeds and submerged tree roots.

The greatest piscean jump I ever saw was achieved by a sea trout who, in its attempt to hurdle a weir, javelined itself about fifteen feet through the air and hit a friend of mine, who was fishing on the weir sill, right in the middle of his chest. He almost fell over, more in shock than because of the impact, but the fish seemed remarkably unaffected and, after a moment's pause, flipped itself safely back into the weir pool, just ahead of my friend's grasping hands.

Thinking about aerialized fish makes me wonder

just how much the level would drop if, for some surreal reason, every fish in the river leapt simultaneously out of the water. Being an astonishingly species-rich habitat, I guess it would, momentarily, go down quite a long way. Just about every kind of British freshwater fish swims in its gently flowing waters. There is still a run of salmon, despite the general decline of this species in the south of England, and there are a fair number of sea trout in the lower reaches as well as colonies of big barbel and more than a few colossal carp. The middle reaches are a haven for roach, perch, bream, pike, chub, dace, brown trout and grayling, and most of these species are still present, albeit in lesser numbers, in the upper stretches, along with the usual swarms of minnows plus a few nice gudgeon, loach and bullhead.

One of the reasons why the river has such a rich and varied population is the different kinds of terrain through which it flows. It has its source in a thickly wooded valley about twenty miles north-west of here, rising through layers of sand and clay that geologists like to call Jurassic beds. However, before it's had time to wipe the bubbles from its eye or learnt how to run

properly it finds itself trapped by a dam and transformed from infant stream into a rather grand lake,
the centrepiece of an ornamental eighteenth-century
landscape. But even the feeblest riverlet can't be per-
manently contained, and as the water pours down the
lake's spillway it rediscovers its identity, escaping along
narrow channels to follow its ancient course. Growing
in strength and depth as it feeds on side streams,
seasonal springs and other natural seepages it becomes
a small unobtrusive river, meandering quietly through
the landscape it has helped to create these last ten or
so thousand years.

Though the middle section flows over a wide
swathe of chalk, the river can seem quite sullen and
dark when compared to the bright-eyed, quick-flowing
streams that are actually born in the chalk hills to the
north and south of here. Yet it also has an intimacy
that its more beautiful sisters lack and, especially at
this time of year when the water is still at summer
level but the weed is dying back after the first cold
nights of autumn, it has a golden clarity. Later on,
when the ditches are flooded after the winter rains and
the current begins to race, the stream will be as brown

and thick as cocoa, yet just a few miles away the chalk streams will be carrying only a tinge of colour. All down its length the river has to contend with weirs, mill hatches, relief channels and flood defences, all of which alter or deflect the current and control the level and flow. Whenever it slides through inhabited areas it keeps a low profile, having to conform to our ideas of polite society, but when the rains come there is always a murmur of rebellion and if deluge follows deluge, as happened here only a few years ago, then it rises out of its torpor and becomes a marauding dragon, engulfing whole villages.

Where I'm fishing now, the rising ground provides a natural flood defence and the narrow flood plain indicates a clear limit to any idea of cultivation or development. The river, therefore, is allowed to follow its traditional course unimpeded, with looping beds, deep holes, rippling gravel shallows and slow marshy meanderings, the current diverted and broken by sedge-covered islands, peninsulas of tree roots, living reefs of fallen willow. All these things are anathema to the land drainage engineer, who has nightmares about obstructed flow. In the past he was given licence to

31

dredge, canalize and de-nature any river that threat-
ened to misbehave, and though nowadays he's forced
to bite his lip and think holistically, for many once
lovely rivers his re-education came too late. Ten miles
downstream, where the river approaches an historic
market town, the flood defences must be almost as
humiliating as the confines of an artificial lake. And if
I lean over one of the town bridges in these times of
low water and negligible flow I have to remind myself
that, while it might look like a canal, this is still a real
river, a continuous living river without a real beginning
or a real end, whose current is not driven solely by
gravity but also pressure and temperature. It flows not
just on land, but also underground, out into the sea
and across the sky, its concentrated earthbound form
connected to its wayward aerial self by onshore winds
which thread it from the sea back to the uplands
where, at intervals, it falls as rain, regenerating the
springs that rise and flow once more to the sea.

A small tributary to this river has its source in the
hills around my home and yesterday the seventy-foot
well in my garden was officially declared dry for the
first time this century. The stream is still running

because the springs further down the valley remain strong, but because the intervals between rains have become even longer, the minnows and little trout are getting nervous and the kingfishers and herons are getting fat.

The rain will return, however, and maybe sooner than last night's weatherman predicted. The blue of the sky was milky this morning and the sun had water in its eye when it rose. Showers by evening were the forecast, but despite the breeze dropping almost to stillness, the sky, as I write, is filling with high thin cloud – and it can't be midday yet.

FOURTH
CAST

❦

Rumours
of Rain

A river is a consequence of rain. And if it doesn't rain . . .

In the drought year of 1976 rivers, lakes and ponds all over the country began to shrivel and by August I began to hear worrying stories about a much-loved stream that I hadn't fished since childhood. Rumours of its suffering made me hurry to its side only to find that it had vanished. What I'd known as an enchanted river had mutated into a potholed lane, as if my memory of it had been nothing but a convincing fantasy. Where the water used to flow was now just a strip of sun-bleached stones that zigzagged away into a heat-hazed distance. I started walking down the middle of it, following the contours of all the little depressions and ridges in the places I used to fish. Here and there were still a few puddles. Wherever shading trees hung over the outside of bends, unconnected pools of shallow water trembled with the activity of little fish, mostly loach and bullheads, but there were no deeper trenches that might have provided sanctuary to the larger species. What had happened to them all? Had the local badgers and foxes been feasting as much as the herons, or had the fish managed to survive by following the dwindling flow down to some safer level, like a weir pool or a confluence? Below a bridge was a once famous swim that my friends and I had considered to be bottomless. Walking, slightly bewildered, between the banks, I discovered it wasn't quite the canyon of childhood myth, but when the water had been flowing it must have been fifteen feet deep, which in a small river is almost the same as bottomless.

Finally I came to the sweeping gravelly bend below which I caught my first non-minnow. I was expecting to crunch over the gravel and trudge directly into the woods beyond, but even before I saw the water I heard it – a wonderfully musical trickling as the river – Mole by name, mole by nature – rose up sparkling between the layers of stones. Exactly as the local history books described, the stream had been following a subterranean course – or rather, it had been remade by perennial springs coming in from the surrounding chalk. The water welled forcefully up, forming a cold crystalline pool that stretched from bank to bank and flowed away over the gravel and through the distant trees just like its old self, or like a forgotten dream that I'd suddenly remembered.

One night in mid-September a great storm unrolled across the south of England and the rains finally returned. Despite the late hour, I had to drive immediately to the desiccated riverbed, hoping to watch it in the shining dark rapidly transforming from puddled lane into a raging torrent; but the dots didn't join up till the following day. By then, the puddles were multiplying like cells, expanding and overflowing until there was just one ever-increasing surge.

As I write – and I just missed a tremendous take because I was scribbling and not concentrating – the sky is filling with pale corn-coloured clouds, while over in the north-west something much darker is rising. The showers predicted by the weatherman will certainly be welcome, though the river would probably prefer something more extreme to increase its pulse rate and wash away the clinging remains of summer. The fish, however, don't want a deluge as it would send in a sea of run-off from the recently ploughed fields upstream, putting them into a gush of mud soup. What both I and the fish would like is a prolonged period of gently falling rain to sweeten the water and gradually bring everything back to its proper level and pace. In the meantime a cool shower might just be enough to sharpen the fishes' appetite.

Perch are big-eyed sight feeders who get very sniffy about cloudy water. The reason they prefer this middle stretch of the river to the clay-bedded upper reaches is because of the chalk through which pure clear alkaline water rises from deep aquifers. And not only does a bright stream make for easier pickings, it also makes for brighter perch. In muddy or clay-tinged water the perch has a dull colour with indistinct markings, but in transparent depths he looks as if he's just been painted.

Last October, when the river was deeper but still almost as clear as it is now, I was walking slowly downstream looking for a new casting place when I saw a shower of minnows burst through the surface a split second ahead of a huge upswirl. The disturbance was too big for anything other than a pike, but as it subsided I glimpsed a broad striped flank that seemed to light up like neon and then disappear again into the swirl. I would never have spotted it had it not been so brilliantly marked, but I presumed a pike must have been pursuing it as it pursued the minnows. Another silver cascade of minnows preceded a less explosive boil and, having inched closer to the water's edge, I was able to clearly see what was happening. There was no pike and not one but three very large perch harrying the minnows like a trio of tigers pursuing rabbits. Even though the sun wasn't directly on the water, the fish looked magnificent in their hunting – all flared fins, strong colours and glittering flanks. They made several individual attacks, scattering the shoals, but then converged in a series of fluid yet seemingly uncoordinated assaults, sweeping the minnows along in a single column and either chasing them into the nearby weed beds or forcing them spectacularly upward into my element. The frenzy lasted only about a minute, then the perch folded themselves up and sank gracefully down to the riverbed, lying together in the current looking as harmless and distinctive as a group of zebras. But it was only because I had actually watched them descend that I was able to continue observing them. If I took my eyes off them for a second the black backs and barred flanks dissolved into near invisibility and it took a while to relocate them.

All I can see in this pool, if I cautiously stand up and look towards the far bank, is the black tail of the same chub that's been drifting just below the surface for maybe two hours, maybe longer. Now the sun has gone behind cloud there is no means of telling the time, and I don't want to know either. I never wear a watch and, anyway, our perception of time as an orderly sequence of regular ticks and tocks has no relevance here in the alternative dimension that is fishing.

At the moment my time is corresponding with the slow stealthy approach of what is surely a rain cloud; but the distant hills remain just as clear as they were when I arrived, five hours or five days ago. Yet the breeze is dropping and the air is changing, but not cooling, which is just as well because if the promised rain was coming in on a cold front I'd be pessimistic. Perch, like all freshwater fish, respond gloomily to a sudden drop in temperature if it's followed by cold heavy rain. If anything, the temperature has risen a degree or two and, perhaps as a result of this, the air is filling with ghostly columns of dancing flies. As the fly hatch continues, everything around me seems to be livening up. The swallows are rising a little higher, snatching the insects in flight rather than skimming them off the surface, and a flock of long-tailed tits is twittering out of the alder and up into the willow behind me. The way they thread themselves into the light breeze reminds me of a shoal of minnows working delicately against the current, while the swallows' flight resembles the way dace plane effortlessly through the flow.

One of the flies – a large dark olive, I think – has landed on the top of my pen as I'm writing. There you are, little fly; I dedicate this line to you. And maybe I'll be able to dedicate a beautiful perch to you as well because, unfortunately, as your sisters and brothers emerge on the surface, so the fish are beginning to enthusiastically sip them back down again. They're only small fish – little dace and baby chub – but the splashy activity is likely to rouse something more substantial.

The most stupendous perch in the country may be concealed beneath that overhanging tree. Possibly this is where Jason caught his monster which, of course, he returned to grow even bigger so that some other lucky angler might one day happen upon it. Although I'm sure I'm in the presence of perch, what I need now is a sign, something to finally confirm my belief. Perhaps this fly on my pen will lead me to it. And, meanwhile, the light sinks a shade darker as the sky-wide cloud reaches over me.

FIFTH
CAST

*The
Chaos
Theory of
Angling*

The problem with something as subtle as the instinctive sense is that it can be so drowned out by the demands and distractions of everyday life that its soft voice is rarely heard. Even when the messages do get through they are often ignored because they sometimes require us to act spontaneously and no one is allowed to do anything until they have read the instructions. But fishing offers a dimension where, even if you don't cast very far into it, you can be free of the wired-up world and suddenly in touch with an equally complex, less concise but deeper-rooted reality. The simpler your approach the more intimately you're involved; uncluttered by a barrow load of equipment, untroubled by the passage of time, hopefully undisturbed and often unambitious, you rediscover the art of improvisation that you mastered as a child, and as you become more absorbed in the watery surroundings you begin to notice details – the bending of a reed, the forming of a ripple, an abrupt stillness – that gradually join up to create an event that you may become part of. This is, however, just an elementary decoding of the clues, the first stage in the retuning of the senses. Only later, after more experience, can the code be read unconsciously, just by a glimpse. And even then, just to add to the interest, you can set out on a perfect day and unaccountably lose touch completely as if the batteries in a radio had just died. Suddenly there's no signal and you will have to rely solely on guesswork and your own angling ability.

I can resign myself to those times when, for some reason, I'm either too slow to take in the hints around me or too dull – and I can even enjoy those occasions because then I have no expectation, no vision and can therefore happily idle the whole day away, letting the river prattle on about absolutely nothing. It can however be something of a disappointment when my gut feeling has brought me to a place and a time where I can almost touch the fins of my dream only to have it all snatched away at the last moment.

Just before the hills to the north-west began to go grey behind a curtain of rain, I decided that as everything else was more active, I should be, too. I reeled in, attached an amber-tipped goose quill to the line, shotted it, re-baited and re-cast, feeling absurdly confident as the float sailed down towards the tree. Despite the lack of chances during the previous hours, I honestly expected the quill to vanish instantly and suffered a mild sense of betrayal when it didn't. I cast again and then again, the orange tip looking lovely as it drifted through the grey-green reflections of the leaves; but each time I experienced the same incredible nothing.

The continuing fly hatch made me wonder if something else was happening down the food chain. Maybe the caddis and shrimp colonies had been so excited by the change in conditions they'd thrown caution to the current and come out from under their stones to play. The perch, therefore, were possibly too busy gathering mouthfuls of river bugs to notice a passing worm. Or maybe they were suspicious of it as it was the only worm in the crowd.

There was another hint that the larger fish might have gone down to feed, when I noticed that the chub had disappeared. But one kind of thing leads to another . . .

A new weather system had created a raincloud; the oncoming rain plus a change in pressure had activated the insects; the insects had activated the normal-sized fish and they in turn attracted the attentions of a crocodile-sized pike that is now fanging about in my pool casting his grisly shadow over my hopes.

I was watching my float trickle downstream again when a half-dozen silver fish – roach and dace – exploded into the air just ahead of it. For a moment I wondered whether I was witnessing the arrival of a giant perch, but then I saw the long lithe green monster. It swirled heavily and juggernauted upstream, making a big bulge in the surface before sinking menacingly under the bank below me.

When I say 'monster' I should qualify that by saying it *seemed* monstrous in this part of the river. To be fair, it was about a yard long and might have weighed eighteen pounds. But it was much too big and predatory for me.

So was that it? Had I arrived at the sweetest perch pool only to have it savaged by an even more diabolical presence than my own? I didn't cast again, but watched as the pike reappeared below me, hanging motionless in the current and seeming to look me straight in the eyes.

Should I just creep away before the rain came and start again tomorrow? I didn't think the pike had begun to fish in earnest yet: both of us were just sizing the place up. But while the inhabitants had obviously been indifferent to me, the pike's reputation alone was enough to freeze a leech's blood. And though a perch with its armoured fins could out-swagger most dangers, it would surely have found itself chomped in two had it swaggered just then.

The rain was suddenly a field's distance away and so I didn't go looking for another pool. I certainly wasn't going to go home, not with at least half a day left yet, so I'm still here, hunkered down and finishing this page now as the first drops splat across it.

★

There was wind as well as rain – and just before the squall hit me a hundred rooks spiralled out of the field opposite looking like the flying debris in a tornado. Now, maybe twenty minutes later, I'm damp, but I haven't got that clinging wet chill down my back that signifies a proper soaking. It was a deluge, but just brief enough not to drown me. My hat and coat were almost equal to it, but my notebook, which was in my pocket, feels like a squidged slice of bread. The cloud is breaking up, although the light is still subdued and there's no doubt more rain to follow – which I should be happy about. It seems at the moment as if the rain is still falling, but it's only the dripping of leaves.

Obviously such a short intense shower has made not the slightest difference to the look of the water, but I think the fish might've enjoyed it. I'm looking out for the pike but I can't see whether it's still brandishing itself. Perhaps its appearance had nothing to do with the conditions. Large pike on a small river move around a good deal, like a hood keeping an eye on his particular manor, and this villain was probably just stopping off at one of his favourite ambush sites. However, because it fits more neatly into my chaos theory, I shall continue to believe that its presence had nothing to do with routine and was instead the end result of an inexorable domino effect.

Although fishes are generally predictable in their habits, as anglers are in theirs, there is no telling how a fishing day is going to unfold. The fact that angling is a chancy business is one of its greatest appeals – especially in today's regulated world. Even without the workings of the chaos principle, the angler has to work with changeable weather, the moodiness of the fish, the state of the water, the proximity of other anglers, the arrogance of swans, the blindness of dogs and their owners, the obstinacy of cattle. Unlike other watery activities, like boating or swimming, a whole day can pass without anything seeming to happen. Unlike non-watery activities, like tennis, cricket or football, fishing does not conform to straight lines or strict rules: its only essential rules are moral ones and, anyway, it's not a game or a sport but a genetic imperative that makes us whole again each time we give it expression.

To make it more understandable to my non-angling friends, I sometimes say that fishing is a bit like chess, but however infinite the combination of moves, the pieces in chess are always the same. And sometimes I say it's a bit like poker, but however the cards are dealt they are always the same cards. In fishing there are no constants – unless you fish in a goldfish bowl or one of those densely stocked carp or trout ponds, which is the same thing. One of the delights and frustrations of a river is that it frequently reshuffles your hand in mid-cast and however perfect or clumsy your technique, however wily or stupid the fish, the river will often have the final say – unless, like today, some other unexpected current adds itself to the flow.

As a scientific hypothesis, the chaos theory proposed that the draught from a butterfly's wing could initiate a chain of events stretching across continents culminating in a violent storm on the other side of the planet; but while a manic meteorologist might possibly trace the course of today's downpour all the way back through a sequence of ever-decreasing reactions to the moment when a woman flung open a window in Melbourne, the type of chaos visited upon anglers usually has a more localized origin and nothing to do with the weather. For instance, while fishing an ancient pond in the Black Mountains, I once witnessed a perfect chain of disruptive events without even having to turn my head. I was stalking a big wild carp that was feeding along the edge of a weed bed and my piece of floating crust was less than a yard from its surface-sniffing nose. It was mid-summer: all around the pool sheep grazed the grass and groups of lambs trotted from bank to bank, curious about the look of the water. The only disturbance to the tranquil pastoral was an occasional faint 'whump' from some distant quarry blasting. The vibrations didn't seem to disturb my carp, but just as it approached the crust there was a slightly heavier blast. While my fish seemed once again indifferent, there was a reaction elsewhere. As the dull sound echoed around the pool, a previously unseen carp leapt high into the air. It was so close to the water's edge it must've splashed the group of lambs at that moment standing almost next to it. Completely startled, they galloped off round the pool, and though their little feet were hardly thunderous there were enough of them to cause quite a rumble as they passed me. They certainly caused more commotion than the quarry blasting and the big carp swept away into deeper water and didn't return. But would it have panicked had I not been present?

Last month, at another, much larger carp water, I was stalking a group of fish who always managed to keep just out of casting range, despite the fact that I avoided skylining myself by creeping along on all fours through a dense reed bed. I kept having to change positions, while the fish gently drifted into shallower and shallower water. Eventually I seemed to have them where I wanted them, because the water became so shallow, and some of them were so big – well over thirty pounds – they couldn't proceed any further. They settled down and began to feed, possibly a hundred yards from me, but as I began to crawl to within casting distance, keeping my head down all the time, I heard a weird rushing sound and looked up to behold a fantastic sight. Heading towards me was a tidal wave – a tsunami of carp – surging back down the lake. There was foam and stirred-up mud and maybe seventy or eighty huge fish, many of them leaping like dolphins as they swept onward. I've not seen anything like it in fifty years of fishing and could not fathom what was happening until, after a few moments, I felt rather than heard a deep pulsing throb. Looking skyward I eventually spotted the tiny dot of an approaching helicopter, flying slowly over the valley. Water is a perfect conductor for low-frequency sound and the carp had obviously detected the distant vibrations long before anything else. But would they have found it so unbearable had I not been squirming through the reeds?

The proximity of other anglers often triggers a chaotic sequence, as a friend of mine discovered when he was casting over a brown trout in a narrow chalk stream. Twice the fish had risen and almost taken his mayfly and my friend guessed it was going to be third time lucky. But then another angler, fishing upstream, hooked a tree on the opposite bank. He, too, had been trying to tempt a large trout, but he spoilt his chances when the dead branch he had hooked snapped and fell virtually on top of his fish, which bolted downstream, straight through my friend's pool, taking his trout with it. Perhaps, though, his trout would only have slipped to one side had he not been on the bank.

No matter how cautiously you approach the river, you will be noticed. And although you may only disturb a little dabchick, there will be consequences because the fish register even the slightest disturbance on their Richter scales. Initially, they may not visibly react; however any additional sudden movement or vibration will cause their internal needles to flicker and then all it takes is a slightly clumsy footfall and the needles swing into the red zone. Perhaps only one fish will sidle away into cover, but all the rest will drift lower in the water, and follow every subsequent move you make, perfectly aware of what it is that is parting the reeds above their heads. Even if you disappeared for an hour, it wouldn't make any difference because, whatever the biologists say, fish do remember, at least in the short term. Once they've twigged you it doesn't matter how much lower you keep your profile; if anything else perplexes them it will be used as evidence against you, whether it be lambs running, a helicopter droning over, a fish panicking, or a butterfly opening its wings against the sun.

SIXTH
CAST

❧ ⸎ ❧

Reality
Bites

After weeks without a drop of rain, any reasonable shower will make a landscape delicious with scents, especially here in September when, despite the drought, these uncultivated fields were already smelling like a herb garden. If the sky clears before sunset we will have, also as a consequence of the rain, ribbons of pure white mist. And whatever happens for the rest of the day, whether a clearing sky or a monsoon, it won't be anything other than pure and beautiful because I've just caught this fish and now everything has been lit up by it.

It didn't matter that I never got to see whether the

pike was still here because, quite suddenly, it seemed that it wasn't; or if it was, it had eaten its lunch and slunk off into a dragonish slumber. As the partying of the surface-feeding fish had been pooped by the pike's monstrous gatecrashing, so the ending of the shower and the predator's apparent departure signalled another rippling of activity. Dace began to sip at the surface, a small chub made a splashy grab for something, minnows flipped themselves into the air. Perhaps some of these fish were simply expressing a lively reaction to the re-oxygenated water, perhaps some were keeping out of the way of another smaller (if more handsome) predator, but I think most were either mopping up the last of the fly hatch or snatching the insects that had been shot down out of the trees by the rain. The river was a moving scroll of small outspreading silver circlets.

It seemed a good moment for a re-cast. Picking up the rod again, I gave it a rap with my knuckles to knock the droplets from it, re-baited and flicked the quill out into midstream. There was an instant response, which seemed almost unbelievable after such an interminably slack line – the float zipping under before it had properly settled. When I upped with the rod tip, however, the cane curved only a few degrees and I reeled in a splashy big-mouthed chub of about a pound. The next cast produced an identical fish – it could have been the same one – but the third and fourth casts were barren, which was somehow reassuring. I missed a tiddling kind of bite on the fifth run down and then for several subsequent casts I simply watched an orange float recede into the near distance. Maybe ten possibly twenty minutes passed before the moment arrived – but I knew it was coming because the river made it clear that the flow was with me. The more I settled into it, the slower the quill flew through the air when I cast, the more delicately it landed, the easier my control of the reel as the float sailed downstream, the less the tiddlers bothered me, the more prepared I was for the final convergence. A true expert could never have attained that level of mad certainty. I wasn't even surprised when the quill jiggered and sank – quite slowly – only halfway towards the slanting tree; but when a steady resistance increased to an unstoppable charge I shouted 'Whoa!' which proves I wasn't being completely blasé.

As a far distant hawk can be identified by its flight pattern, so an unseen fish on the line has a recognizable signature in its down strokes and tail swipes. I can usually tell a chub by the way its initial dash culminates in a series of sharp angular plunges, and I know a trout by the way it dashes and keeps dashing. A bream gives itself away by finning determinedly but then pretending to be a paper bag, while a barbel powers off and then locks down. Large grayling offer a curious resistance that is solid yet serpentine, but the serpentine eel swings around like a windmill. Nothing runs as insanely far as a salmon and nothing runs as cunningly far as a carp. Tench have a throbbing tugboat determination, while a roach's fin stroke is more delicate and fluid. A big perch will normally hold firm for a moment as if sizing up the situation before beginning a routine of weaving, jagging rushes, which was not what my fish was doing. The dive down the pool seemed reminiscent of a chub except the rhythm of the tail stroke was definitely perch-ish. There was, of course, the possibility that I'd hooked a fleet-finned pike – maybe *the* pike – but it didn't have a pike's terrifying acceleration and I told myself not to be so pessimistic.

Before anything else could happen, however, I had to reel myself in from a crisis. The fish had taken the line beneath the alder and I could feel the downreaching branches fingering it. There was a tense pause, with nothing yielding and me holding the light twelve-foot rod so that the tip was pushed underwater to keep the tackle clear of trouble. The action of the submerged cane muddled the sensations running up the line – for a moment I wondered if the fish had driven me into the roots – but then the pressure both eased and became more animated, making the bend in the rod less painful to look at. Hope and line came back to me, winding up to the sublime moment when I saw, deep down, the vision I'd been waiting for – unmistakable, bold and bright, like a banner showing black bands on a field of gold – the flank of a large perch.

'Gently now,' I said as, with my left hand, I reached for the net while, with my right, I brought the fish to the surface. The way it hoisted its big dorsal – an expression of defiance – reinforced the martial image, but it came fairly quietly over the mesh and I heaved it up and laid it carefully down in wet grass.

Out of the water, the flame-red of the tail and underfins was even more striking than the array of stripes, also the flanks were more green than gold; but I was, at first, too bowled over by the occasion to appreciate the creature properly and it was only after I'd weighed and photographed it – such an undignified ritual (it was just over three pounds) – that I really looked at it properly. Getting a firm but even grip around its shoulders, I leaned over the bank and held it for a long minute in the current. Its mouth took in gillfuls of water and its fins spread out angrily again. When I slowly turned it on its side it wallowed in my hands but didn't try and burst free.

Despite the metallic sheen and the grooved armour-plated head, the overall texture, the blaze of colours and the markings gave the impression of plumage rather than scaling, as if it was half bird. The eye was also bird-like – large and black – and its head had a hawkish profile. It stirred, relaxed its fins, but then spread them once more – a bird in the hand. However, though I was only holding it lightly, it seemed to sense that it wasn't in danger and could glide off whenever it liked. With its guard down it didn't appear quite as grandiose as when I first glimpsed it; the colours, close up, looked more subtle and varied – soft ochres, pale blues, deep ambers and every shade of green. When I tilted it to the light it shimmered gold and when I opened my hands it hung for a moment in the current before swooping down, merging rapidly into the colours of the river.

SEVENTH
CAST

*Nostalgia
for the
Perch*

The scent of perch on my hands weaves me along the overgrown bankside to the pond of my childhood where my fishing began. As an eleven-year-old learning how to fish I was not of course bothered nor normally conscious of any of the smells associated with my new favourite occupation. Furthermore, if I'd thought about such an olfactory subject it would have been based on the premise that all fish from stickleback to shark smell exactly the same. Yet each species has a subtly different fragrance and although some, given the same habitat and the same feeding habits, are difficult to sniff apart, fish with different diets, like the pike and perch, have a distinct air about them. The pike has a sharp steely tang, while the scent of a perch is spicier – evidence of a more varied diet.

I may not have deliberately sniffed at a perch, but I became familiar with their special piquancy because my dreams began to absorb it.

Being less concerned then than I am now about the welfare of fishes, I used to put even the tiniest perch into a small keepnet, and though this would inevitably result in scoured scales and frayed fins it afforded me the pleasure, when releasing them at the day's end, of admiring my catch a second time. I would watch them swim away, but could also take more than their memory home because their distinctive smell could cling to the mesh for days, much to my mother's disgust. She would make me hang the net from a tree at the bottom of the garden, but being a new and wildly enthusiastic fisherboy I had to have all my angling accoutrements secure in my own room; which meant that, come morning, the net would be mysteriously hanging from a hook next to my bed, and all night I would have been breathing wonderfully evocative air.

The first fish I ever caught was a gudgeon, four inches short, purple and speckled; but in the village pond there were almost as many perch as gudgeon and though they were mostly the same size and just as easy to outwit they were the precursors of the fabulous monsters that I used to hear about. A gudgeon could never be anything other than a tiddler, but some of these perch, according to local legend, weighed *over a pound* and the idea of such a creature turned every cast, no matter how bungled, into a prayer. It was the perch, therefore, rather than gudgeon that made me feel like a true angler, and of course the first one was a major event. I remember thinking that something momentous was about to happen when my float wobbled sideways in an unfamiliar manner. I waited a second, then whisked a miraculous sparkle through the air, catching it and holding it for probably too long in the palm of my hand – amazed by its bristling reality, impressed by the definitely painful spines on the gill covers and along the dorsal fin. Once I'd got the hang of them, I was able to catch them quite regularly, but they never lost their dazzle; and despite the fact that they were not much longer than my finger there was always the wild thought that eventually the float would go down and nothing would flutter towards me because I'd hooked something too big to fly.

Because none of my family or friends had any interest in angling, my first few years on Earth, before I'd held a rod, were spent in ignorance of the great truth that man was born to fish. Therefore the names of almost all the freshwater fish were not part of my limited vocabulary and the word 'perch' only had one meaning: it was what birds did. I was vaguely aware that it was also something to do with an obscure measurement, but its association with water was unknown to me until the autumn of 1958, the year before my first cast, when I joined a school trip to Hampton Court Palace. My class was treated to an interminable guided tour round the grand chambers of Henry VIII, from where two friends and I managed to escape, slipping out of a 'staff only' side entrance and disappearing into the wide open spaces of the park. Actually, only I ran into the park; my two pals headed straight for the café, eager for ice cream; but I'd seen a pale sheet of water extending beyond tall ornamental railings and I wanted to have a closer look. I found a gate, opened it and went over to the bankside of an astonishing-looking lake. It was formal in shape, long and narrow, reed-fringed, lily-studded and bordered with two avenues of ancient trees which accentuated its perspective so that it seemed to be slanting uphill. The Longwater outshone anything I could've seen in the confines of the palace, but it had yet more to offer.

The day was dull and damp and there was no one else in the scene apart from the figures of two young anglers fishing in a gap between lily beds about forty yards away. Although, like me, they didn't appear to be doing anything other than staring at the water, there was an undeniable purpose to their idleness. While I would soon have to give myself up to the justifiable tirade of verbal abuse, these two much older boys could remain in paradise all day. While I felt guilty and self-conscious standing alone on the bankside in my school uniform, no one would even raise an eyebrow about them, validated as they were by their fishing rods.

Just before I rejoined my party, I went over to them and asked if they'd caught any fish. 'Some nice perch,' said one of them.

There was a keepnet in the water, something I'd once seen at my local pond, and the 'nice perch' were just visible as greenish black-banded shapes, fidgeting back and forth and poking their noses into the mesh. My heart went out to them, not because of their plight but because of their mystery.

'Can I see them out of the water?'

But the boys explained that lifting the net would cause too much disturbance, spoiling the chances of any more fish.

Any *more*! Blimey! Despite none of the perch being longer than a hand's length, there must've been at least half a dozen. Truly, these were master anglers. Maybe they were members of a Royal Society of Anglers that dated back to the lake's creation: Perch Anglers by Appointment to the Monarchy.

I left them to their endeavours and walked back towards ignominy and certain detention, not that I cared anymore about such trifles. I had learnt a new and significant meaning to a familiar word and now the verb would always be secondary to the noun. Furthermore, I'd realized how simple it was for a boy – for anyone – to be free.

EIGHTH
CAST

*The
Journey
Back to
Earth*

The Hampton Court perch incident had a kind of precedent. Four years earlier I had made a similar but even more outstanding discovery that was also linked to ideas of mystery and freedom, though, until I was marched off for my first day at school, freedom was not a concept I needed to think about. It was only when the school gates closed behind me that I began to appreciate my former carefree existence and understand that freedom would now be denied me until I'd learnt how to earn it. But the more exercise books pleaded with me to write something, *anything*, on their blank pages, the more I yearned to escape them – to be free again to explore the world alone or with other boys my age and not be guided by any authoritative hand, to once again find my own way into castles of fallen trees, up mountains of hay bales or over garden walls into other worlds. I also longed to get back to the village pond, a vast expanse of water that I'd only recently circumnavigated in wellington boots, towing my yacht *Endeavour* behind me. During the voyage I had naturally kept a wary eye out for sharks and pirates, but couldn't avoid an encounter with a sea monster that was undeniably and palpably real, if not actually of the sea.

What was it? It had risen up out of the green murk, golden, glittering, stupendous – at least twice as long as the *Endeavour*, and with a fin on its back almost as big as the sail. When I came ashore I asked the local inhabitants if they'd seen it too, but there was only one other who'd witnessed the spectacle and he didn't know what it was either.

There was a distant island that I'd been trying to reach, but the waters around it were too deep and dangerous for my boots. As I looked back towards it, still wobbly after the confrontation, the creature reappeared, its broad back breaking the surface. Incredibly it was joined by several others, all equally immense – and this in a pond I'd been paddling around since the day I'd learned to walk, and where no one had ever before seen anything bigger than a sardine. Splashing and rolling, the giants eventually passed out of sight beneath the forest of willows on the far bank.

For a while afterwards – maybe a week or two – I remained in a state of quiet shock, but then it became necessary to know exactly what kind of creatures they were. Did they have a name? Were they really my own discovery? Did they truly exist or had they just been a trick of the light? I didn't have long enough to find any answers because, shortly afterwards, school closed over me and began to trivialize everything about the world that I'd thought was wonderful, including monsters in ponds.

My early education was concerned mostly with facts and certainties, yet the only fact that mattered to me was that I couldn't see out of the high Victorian windows, and the only certainties that gave me hope were that a bell would ring in the afternoon, the doors would open and I could breathe again. I had never, as

I said, thought about freedom or time or space until school took them away from me, but though I could still savour these things during my daily parole, there was a new wildness about me then that made me lose my sense of direction. The pressure of six hours confinement meant that, at three o'clock, I just wanted to run and run and run. It was the same with all my friends. There had never been any urgency between us before, but once schooling began we were always in a great hurry to do things whenever we were free again. It was almost as if, having discovered what boredom was, we were determined not to let it affect our own world; but the result was that, instead of quietly following our own paths back to the old magic, we got confused and distracted and so never had enough time to get there. The village pond was only a sixty-second run from school, but the new pace of life meant that my patience could never last long enough for the mystery to reveal itself again. I still believed in it, but after a month or two my faith began to waver. So the pond reverted to what it was always good for: a place for throwing stones, for sailing and sinking model boats, for falling into; and the monsters gradually sank down to the same status as the ghost Billy saw in the sweet-shop window and the goblin that Dennis chased into the bracken on the heath.

Time moved busily on, corralled more and more into routines, yet the monsters would still occasionally rise up, usually in the middle of lessons, and I'd find myself adding fish instead of numbers. I once had a vague idea that I might ask one of the anglers who occasionally fished the pond whether they'd ever seen anything unusual, but when, eventually, the opportunity arose I didn't even have the courage to speak to them. They would sit or stand there on the bank, never catching anything or doing anything, yet I found their stillness and seeming alertness quite impressive. It was extraordinary that grown-ups could appear so purposeful and yet remain so quiescent. Perhaps, if I'd had more time to hang around, I would've seen someone reel in one of the little sardine-sized fish that often flickered over the shallows; that would've been exciting – but of course, now I was a schoolboy, I had learned how to be impatient. Also, there were suddenly too many other things to think about, things which my friends insisted I familiarize myself with –

like the names of every cowboy who had ever appeared in a comic or on television, from the Cisco Kid to the Range Rider. We also had to learn the vocabulary of Dan Dare, interplanetary spaceman, as well as Robin Hood and Captain Nemo. Not only did we associate ourselves with these characters, we *were* them. Once the Indian wars had broken out on the heath, usually after school or at weekends, the pond became almost an irrelevance. We might sometimes have galloped round it, but the fighting was so intense there was no time to stop and stare or even give our horses a drink.

When the wars were over we established a space station in the hollows where Dennis had seen the goblin, but almost as soon as interplanetary flights began we realized that the goblin must, in fact, have been a Martian and consequently things became quite sinister, no one daring to approach the space station on their own. We cancelled all package holiday trips to Mars and would only enter its orbit in the Battle Rocket.

During this crisis I was obviously unable to visit the pond, nor did I think about it, but all the while it was lapping innocently at its grassy banks and the unidentified creatures were truffling contentedly in its ooze.

The great enigma was finally resolved during the blissful freedom of my first summer holidays, when I was walking again round the pond, not alone nor with my spacemen friends, but with my father. He was not as amazed as me to discover an old fisherman who appeared to have actually caught something, and, unlike me, father had no hesitation in going quietly up to him and asking him about it. The angler was sitting on a creel, smoking a pipe and watching his float; at his feet was a long tubular net, with wire hoops, extending into the water, and something inside it was stirring. Responding to father's request, the old chap kindly drew in the net until a miraculous fish was half out of the water, wallowing on its side, looking as fabulous as when I first saw it – or one exactly like it – all that mythical time ago. Close to, it seemed terrifyingly huge and strikingly beautiful – its flank evenly covered with large iridescent gold scales, its shape perfectly symmetrical, its fins and tail broad yet fine, almost delicate. It was, said the angler, a carp, and because it had been properly confirmed – almost touched – it was now safe from all those things, like school and alien invasion, that could have destroyed it. *Carp*: the most sublime example of life on Earth that I had ever seen. I wasn't going to be a spaceman any longer.

NINTH
CAST

❧✦❧

*Do
Fish Feel
Rain?*

Maybe an hour since it stopped and the only visible evidence of the rain is in the procession of pale yellow willow leaves knocked out of their trees by the cloudburst and now floating away downstream. Already there are slow almost stationary rafts of them caught up in underbank eddies or behind midstream reed beds. Without any increase in flow they'll continue to pack into the slacks for a while longer until the rafts become islands which will endure for a few days and then disappear as the leaves become water-logged and sink. Next month the leaf flow will multiply with each fresh gust of wind; alder, ash, poplar and oak following after the willow leaves, which will soon all be gone. Hopefully, we should have had some more substantial rain by then, raising the water level, strengthening the flow and sweeping everything – leaves, reeds, lilies and weeds – eastwards towards the sea.

At the moment, the slowly drifting leaves are tracing a complex diagram on the surface, revealing all the variations of current in front of me. Beneath the near bank, a line of them is being deflected by a clump of reeds and they file diagonally towards midstream before being scattered by a quite forceful upwelling. There is, apparently, some deep obstruction and it makes the water roll backwards on itself, but I hadn't really noticed it until now. The river shallows towards the far bank, making the leaves speed up a little before another bed of reeds sends them into a whirl. Half of them remain gently spinning in a perfectly circular eddy, the rest are drawn into a narrow channel between the stems, finally escaping into open water and disappearing round the leaning tree.

In twos and threes, like competing miniature canoes, the midstream leaves chase each other along a straight yet still unpredictable course, some of them occasionally veering left or right as a momentary vortex catches them; a few lucky ones ride an unexpected rising sub-current and accelerate ahead of the rest, while some less lucky individuals are checked and then capsized by a downswirling ripple. But even as I'm writing, the competitors are thinning out and until the next rain or wind there won't be many more to join the flotilla. The surface will soon become almost clear again and one of the shortest migrations of the autumn will end as abruptly as it began.

Migrations everywhere. The swifts have already gone, the swallows are about to follow, and during this last hour I've been hearing a familiar 'churr' call that I don't normally associate with September. The fieldfares are here a month early, arriving from Scandinavia (or wherever it is in the north they've been summering). Perhaps their early arrival is a sign of a hard winter to come. If I'm lucky I might see an osprey stopping off for a bite to eat on its long flight to Africa, something I've witnessed several times in previous autumns. A short while ago I saw a cormorant, though luckily it was flying over quite high and didn't look as if it was about to land. A cormorant is a different class of fish eater to an osprey and has been on a different kind of journey. Unlike the seasonal comings and goings of the rest of the avian population, the cormorant's migration has been happening over a period of twenty-five years. Before that time I rarely saw them on rivers or lakes, but because the ecology of our coastal waters has been almost destroyed by pollution and unregulated commercial fishing, the cormorant has had to head inland or die of starvation. If all stretches of river were similar to this one, the voracious fish eater would not have prospered so well. Where the stream is narrow and fallen or leaning trees provide the fish with tangled sanctuaries, the cormorants can't get an easy lunch, but where the river is broader, and tidy-minded people keep the bankside clear of obstructions, the fish have no escape. Nowadays, because the black pirates have established themselves so successfully inland – and how they love the shallow, overstocked, saucer-shaped day-ticket ponds that are the cormorant supermarkets – their population has increased, while, having been gobbled up at the rate of two pounds a day per bird, species like roach and dace are in steep decline in some areas. If they were only troubled by cormorants, it might not be so worrying, but a fish's life is never easy – and then there are anglers!

The floating leaves have now dwindled to a few drifting stragglers and the fieldfares have headed on upstream. In the meantime the clouds have darkened again, which is not what I was expecting after the grey seemed to be thinning steadily back to blue. Because the sky has remembered how to rain, it's obviously decided to do it once more. In fact I can see the distant hills going ghostly under the advancing second wave. The breeze, however, is still slow. If I hurried I could probably reach Jason's cottage before the weather and have a cup of tea. Alternatively, I could stay here and enjoy the novelty – after this parched season – of another soaking. Also, I'm thinking that if one shower can stir a three-pounder, what will two showers do? Hot tea or cold rain? If I deliberate on these profound questions for long enough I know I'll reach that happy moment when the answers will arrive without me. And so, even as I'm considering the matter, the rain cloud has sneaked up on me and the surface of the river is beginning to shimmer under its first touch. It's more mist than rain and it makes only a faint hiss as it falls. If I keep my notebook tucked in close my penning won't dissolve for a while.

I wonder what the drizzle sounds like beneath the surface. Do the fish hear it or feel it? They have no ears, or at least no external ears, but along each flank runs a line of sensory receptors – the lateral line – that detects vibrations, pressure waves and minute electrical pulses, making the side of a fish like a sensitive radar dish. Light rain probably makes a soft ringing along the lateral line that the fish recognize instinctively, while heavy rain must drown out almost every other kind of external stimuli. Particularly in shallow water, a deluge must be a numbing experience, which is why, on those rare occasions when I have been able to observe fish in those conditions, I see them lying very still on the bottom, their fins down almost in a gesture of surrender. Furthermore, while the vibrations of rain must obscure the presence of any waterborne predator, the visual effect of rain across the surface must blind a fish to any threat from above. During a sustained torrent, therefore, fish tend to sink into rain-induced torpor and the chances of catching anything other than pneumonia are unlikely, though of course there are exceptions. However, it's the period immediately after rain that raises an angler's hopes . . .

In the grey light, with a grey background of trees softened by the thin grey curtain of rain, the dazzling colours of a fast low-flying kingfisher sting the optic nerves (the shrill double whistle made me look up).

However fish feel rain, their finely tuned response to it brings me back to all those other things that must affect, disturb and trouble them. Inevitably, I must ask myself how much offence I cause them. I may be using a small barbless hook, fine line and a delicate-tipped rod, but I have just cheated a beautiful perch out of its natural element and no doubt it feared the worst, not realizing that I only wanted it to feed my dream rather than my family. Whatever it thought was happening, the fish obviously objected to it, resisting my advances once it had taken my offering. Having watched big perch scrunching little perch – spines and all – and having seen them crunching huge American crayfish – claws and all – I am at least convinced that all they feel through their mouth is resistance and not pain.

Moreover, though the concentrated pressure must be alarming, as if the worm had truly turned, a hook is probably must less shocking to a fish than the first sensation of a bit and bridle is to a horse.

Because they have a non-circulatory system, fish can withstand and quickly recover from all kinds of terrible ravages, from heron stab to pike gnash – wounds that would prove fatal to a similar-sized mammal – but I dutifully accept that, however tough and resilient they are, fish do not approve of being hoiked out of the water. Of course I never fail to offer a heartfelt apology for disrupting their day, and though they are unimpressed by my words, it's always a joy to release them again simply because of the way the fish spreads its wings as it rediscovers its freedom and glides back to the life it presumed was lost. Sometimes, when the water is clear and not too deep, I've occasionally observed how a fish hangs for a few moments in the current, taking in oxygen before quietly slanting down and beginning to feed once more, as if nothing untoward had happened. And there have been instances when a released fish rejoins its shoal only for me to unintentionally re-catch it a few casts later –

identification is usually straightforward as no two fish are exactly the same. However, although instant recaptures are unusual, the fact that longer-term recaptures occur regularly proves how little effect angling must have on scaled society.

Back in 1973, I caught a carp of thirty-eight pounds from Redmire Pool in Herefordshire. Seven years later I caught it again, by which time it had grown into what was then the biggest carp in Britain – a fifty-one-pounder. And because the fish had a unique scaling pattern, photographic records confirm that this carp had also been caught in 1959. No doubt the fish was suitably dismayed when it met me the second time, but its various encounters had obviously not undermined its robust good health.

I frequently have to explain my passion to my dry friends and then I find myself reeling off these examples of angling's relative harmlessness. Most of them, however, remain unconvinced, not because of the ethical arguments, but simply because they believe that fishing must be a pointless exercise if you don't eat the fish you catch.

Then I must go back to the very beginning again

and tell them how, when I discovered fishing, the world started to articulate for me in a language I could understand. For the first time in my life I knew exactly what I should be doing without anyone telling me. However, the most important part of this new experience was the actual physical contact with a wild creature: a genuine connection with nature. It was real, but also magic, because I had to somehow conjure it up from the strange depths of my village pond. It was, therefore, a curious but beautiful alchemy: first the hoped-for dream, then the dream transformed into a small flickering fish that rooted me to the Earth. I couldn't transcend that moment by eating what I'd caught and it seemed only fair, having stolen its magic, that I should allow my fish its freedom again.

'Yes,' my dry friends say. 'That's all very nice. But you're not a child anymore. Why do you still *have* to go fishing?'

Because I don't want to lose touch with reality.

TENTH
CAST

*The
Time
Being*

When I look upstream and see everything flowing towards me it's like looking into the
future; when I face downstream and see everything
flowing away, it's like looking into the past. What
makes fishing so compelling, however, is the way it
keeps my attention fixed on the present.

Preferring to travel light, I don't waste much time
pondering technical issues, concentrating instead on
solving the angling puzzle through observation, gradually immersing myself in my surroundings until my
focus narrows to the point where I think I know what
I'm doing. Being happy to keep the act of angling as

simple as possible, I can get down to the slower pace of the natural day, adjusting to a rhythm that has nothing to do with the plodding inevitability of Greenwich Mean Time – or, in this instance, British Summer Time.

Being a reasonably responsible (single) parent of four children I do possess an alarm clock for those days when I have to be home to meet the school bus (not today, thankfully) but, as I said earlier, I do not possess a watch and even if I did it would be made redundant here. Being so absorbed in the present moment I soon lose track of the average hour yet can instead appreciate a different perception of time as I fish through moments that are sometimes astonishingly stretched and others that are impossibly condensed. These variables are usually in accord with whatever is happening, but occasionally they are mysteriously out of kilter and you have an active day full of incident, with the river flowing urgently past you, and yet discover the infinite time of your childhood.

Subconsciously you might synchronize with any of the different rhythms, currents and pauses going on around you. Although concentrating on your fishing, you instinctively notice the changes in the air, the approach of cloud shadows, the rise and fall of natural background sounds, the movement of the sun and water, the flinching of the tiddler shoals; and according to your mood or your sensitivity on the day you might be gradually drawn to one of these more than the others. As each element conforms to its own time you can therefore find yourself unwittingly falling into step, mesmerized by the slowness of one, hustled by the restlessness of another. There is nothing quite so lulling as the look of a painted float poised on the edge of a lily bed in a tench pond at dawn. But time can accelerate suddenly if the fish decide to go on a binge, and an angler can flounder in his attempts to keep up, as happened to me (not for the first time) last June.

I'd been watching my float since sunrise as it sat in calm deep water and I was marvelling at the way it kept separating from and then rejoining its reflection on the lake's gently trembling surface. For an hour at least, probably two, I contentedly waited until the float went down and its reflection rose up. There was a short pause while I considered this phenomenon. The physics of a float does not allow it to suddenly sink;

therefore I presumed something mystical must have occurred. Then realization tapped me on the head and I made a clumsy grab for the rod, seeing, even as I struck, the float reappear. Of course I'd missed the fish. It was as if I had been waiting on a station but had become so engrossed by the perspective of the railway lines that I hadn't noticed my train had come in. But then lots of trains began coming in one after another.

Just after I'd re-cast, the corner of the lake began to fizz with tench bubbles, something I hadn't seen at that water for years. I'd sprinkled the area with cunningly spiced corn and as the fish were obviously going for it there was a rare chance that I might get more than the usual solitary specimen. Yet having been initially flummoxed by the change of pace, it became obvious that any more opportunities were only there to tantalize and frustrate me. I prematurely struck at the next dip of the quill, bungled my next cast and couldn't even put a grain of corn on the hook properly.

Two coot patrols converged from either side of the float and began a major conflict directly in front of me. By the time they'd agreed a truce I guessed it was too late for the tench because by then the climbing, brightening sun would surely have switched them off. I'd missed my opportunities simply because I'd allowed myself to be chivvied into snatching at them.

A soft breeze sprang up and began to shuffle the reeds. I sank back disconsolately on my creel, convinced my float would never move again even if I remained at the lake all season – and the next phase of the morning *seemed* like a season, though maybe it was only a clock-length fifteen minutes. I noticed bubbles dotting the surface again. The tench had come back, but having been sedated by the gently swaying reeds I had all the time in the world to carefully bait my hook, choose my spot and effortlessly cast to it, drawing the line almost taut before preparing for the inevitable response. How satisfying it was to feel a solid connection after the float had slid gracefully away; how superb it was to see the curve of the rod and the line cutting through the ripples; how sweet it was to watch the glistening green of a big tench as it rolled into the net.

Time's elasticity can either advance an angler's cause or threaten to destroy it. I was fishing for barbel on a weir pool one moonlit night and decided to attempt a forty-yard cast from the weir tail, where I was wading, towards the white water where the fish had been showing. I was using my favourite reel – a 1922 Allcock Aerial – but long casting with a centre pin can be problematic, especially at night. (A centre pin is superior in almost every respect to any other kind of winch except that your casting range is limited. Thirty yards 'straight off the drum' is feasible, but forty is asking for trouble.) My tackle was a 6 hook and a half-ounce bored bullet, my bait half a sausage, and I swept it with a forceful underhand cast towards the foaming surge. Forty yards *is* possible, and I have achieved that distance several times when I was practising and nothing was riding on the outcome. Timing and coordination are key, but these can be disrupted when you are in the presence of large fish – and I had seen several rolling in the broken water during the evening. As the reel became a spinning blur in the moonlight, a loop of line caught the handles, jamming everything in mid-flight, but not before yards of line had somehow spiralled off the drum and formed a wonderful pattern of coils round the rod butt. The tackle hung quiveringly in the air for a microsecond then catapulted backwards, splashing down only ten yards from my waders.

The period that followed while I struggled to disentangle myself seemed longer than the time I normally spend on the river in a year, but it was a matter of honour that I succeeded without breaking the line. The idea of simply tearing free, re-threading and re-tackling would have been too humiliating to even consider.

At last, after the moon had gone through several phases, I untwizzled the last knot and was about to wind in the tackle when I felt a strange tremor on the rod. As I said, timing is the secret when you're using a centre-pin reel, and though I hadn't perhaps appreciated it earlier, my cast, with all its Gothic elaborations, had been perfect. Some mighty river prince was hunting through the tail of the weir, drawing gradually closer as I unravelled my line, and at the precise moment I raised the rod to reel in my bait he said: 'I'll have that!' The tip of the rod walloped over and the reel, silent for so long, began to sing my favourite song.

The river had been steadily rising after two days of

heavy rain. The barbel planed effortlessly across the fast current and held steady for a few moments under the far bank. I should have been more patient and not tried too hard to bring him back to me because as soon as I increased pressure he responded by avalanching downstream.

About sixty yards away was a bridge, and if the fish made it through the arch, where the pace of the current almost doubled, then my luck and my line would almost certainly run out.

'Bring the net!' I yelled, as I galloped downriver. My comrade in rods, Jeff, had been quietly fishing upstream, but I'd disappeared from view by the time he'd reeled in and hurried to where I'd left the landing net. There were two big hawthorns leaning out into the water between my starting point and the bridge. I still don't know how I got round or over or through them in the dark but I must surely have gone faster than the speed of light because, when I began running, the fish was almost under the arch and when I reached the bridge I was ahead of him. The change of pressure made him hesitate and he began to hold steady again in midstream. Jeff reached me a short while later, coming down behind the barbed-wire fence that ran parallel with the bank. I began to gain line and saw a pale flank gleaming on the surface before the fish rolled and swept back into the current.

Jeff clambered over the fence with the net, but barbed wire loves landing nets even more than fishermen's trousers. So once again I was stymied by an almost inextricable tangle. My rod – a lovely piece of well-crafted cane – was bent so much it was about to pop the corks off its handle, yet it wasn't as stressed as me.

'Just tear the bloody thing free!' I shouted. But the fence wouldn't let go without a fight and in the meantime the barbel was circling ominously closer to the point of no return. The two time zones – 'mean' and 'barbed wire' – diverged rapidly and I was stretched between the two. Jeff, concentrating on the wire, did not let my panic fluster him, though whenever I turned to check his progress he looked like someone transfixed over a crossword puzzle.

'I've done it!' he shouted triumphantly, and came skidding down the bank just as the fish curved through the quieter water at my feet. It rolled, kicked up a shower of luminous spray and Jeff raised the net around it. Much to my relief and delight the barbel – an elegant and impressive twelve-pounder – was far too big to slip through the rips in the mesh. We could even see the gold of it in the silver of the moonlight.

ELEVENTH
CAST

※━━━━━━❀❖❀━━━━━━※

*The
Serious
Question
of Tea*

A short while ago I half heard a soft 'tap-tapping' from somewhere downstream, but it was too faint to demand much attention. Now I hear it again – but it's much closer, only thirty feet away in the reed bed on the opposite bank. It is the sound of a little death.

The kingfisher I saw earlier – at least it's probably the same one – is perched on a slanting stem with a freshly caught minnow in its beak. The sound I heard was the bird thwacking the little fish against the stem. With a neat flick of the head, lunch was swallowed and now the minnow had gone to lend its support to the enemy of all the other minnows.

Lunch! I have a flask of green tea only half drunk, a jar of pickled herrings and a chunky piece of bread which is moister than it should be. Because I've been so happily lost in the river I'd almost forgotten to be hungry, but the kingfisher has made me realize that I'm ravenous.

The thing to remember when making a packed lunch is that even the plainest food can taste delectable when you eat on the riverbank, which is why I never or hardly ever bother to make sandwiches. Also there's never enough time to make a proper lunch as my usual fishing day is limited to the hours between the departure of the school bus and its return. (It's against my religion to fish at weekends.) This might seem reasonable as the river is only a few miles from home, but a fishing morning must begin slowly and, once the children have waved goodbye and peace has returned after the routine panic of lost shoes and unfinished homework, the first cup of tea cannot be hurried. Then, after going out for a moment to sniff the air and gauge the weather prospects, I must choose the right float for the day and search through the bundles of rods in each corner of each room until I find the one

I need. By the time I take the net down from the study wall the pace of the morning begins to quicken, particularly if I get a scent of the river from the mesh. It's always aggravating if I suddenly remember the bait tin is empty because it means I have to dig a big hole in the vegetable bed – the drier the weather, the deeper the hole. I always think I'll collect the worms on the evening prior to the day, but I hardly ever do, except when it's raining and I can creep out with a torch and pick them off the lawn.

Finally, when almost everything is piled ready by the front door, the river will be rippling quite loudly in my imagination, making it impossible to even think about such a complex task as sandwich making. So I'll frequently take nothing to eat or drink at all, unless I remember to snatch a few apples on the way out. I only persuaded myself to make a flask of tea this morning because the children have gone to stay with friends until tomorrow, and so I had more time to brew it. Also, the idea of fishing till sunset without tea made me feel slightly fraught.

If I'm going to have a social fishing day, meeting friends on the bankside and doing as much talking as casting, then I'll take a whole tea-making kit, including a Kelly Kettle, a teapot, half a gallon of water, milk (soya), a packet of finest Ceylon, mugs and kindling. I rely on my companions to supply the cake. When I'm fishing alone, however, such accoutrements just weigh me down and I'll forgo the freshly made cup and take green tea in a flask (green keeps better than black in a flask over a long period).

Now that I've had my perch, though, and I'm still buoyed by that happy best-fish-of-the-season bubble, a steaming teapot would have rounded the day off beautifully.

Any teapot looks good on a riverbank, but the best I ever saw belonged to my friend Robert, who produced it from his fishing bag to celebrate the biggest grayling I ever caught. It was an exquisite creature but it somehow paled next to the teapot. Extravagantly decorated, silver and capacious, it looked as if a genie would rise out of the spout if it was rubbed – an idea that seemed worth a try when Robert said he'd recently bought it at a market in Marrakesh. It certainly created an other-worldly brew. Robert had also baked a sumptuous fruitcake but in order to eat it all we had to refill the pot several times, all the while watching the sun going down over the river. So there wasn't enough time left for any more grayling, though had we blanked completely the day would still have been perfect.

Last March, on a different stretch of this same river, I joined a group of friends for what would be our final day of the season. As usual, I arrived an hour after everyone else to find Andrew fishing my favourite swim. Therefore, I thought it wise to dump my tea-making kit next to him, knowing that he'd eventually weaken and allow me to make a few casts there if I made him a good brew. Nothing much was happening. It was damp, misty and cool, but a thrush was singing the first full-voiced song of the spring and we guessed the fish would stir eventually. Hugh was up at the bridge, trying to catch a roach; Jeff, Nick and Andrew were, as I was, more interested in perch, but the perch weren't interested in us. At about four in the afternoon, we gave up trying to catch anything and agreed it was time for tea.

I'd forgotten to bring dry kindling but there are always enough spidery dead twigs under bankside trees and, despite the damp conditions, I eventually got a nice plume of woodsmoke rising. (I know a 'gaz' stove would make life easier, but the tea never tastes so good.) Jeff supplied the cake, and though Andrew soon had four very jovial anglers in his swim, the tea was excellent enough for him not to complain. He didn't even object when someone mentioned that there was probably enough room for another rod, but because we couldn't decide *whose* rod it should be, it was inevitable that, after a bit of a rush and some pushing and shoving, three uninvited floats were competing with Andrew's, all sailing downstream within a yard of one another, but, incredibly, without knitting each other's lines. Unresponsive fish can have a remarkably adverse effect on an angler, dulling his spirit, making him doubt his abilities and causing him to feel animosity towards any other angler who looks more likely than him to catch something. A cup of tea has the power to lift these clouds and restore essential optimism, but such was the quality of that day's brew that my casting was suddenly affected by a kind of bravado that made my comrades wince. Furthermore, my float sailed downstream with an admiral's swagger, and I made the dangerous claim that it didn't matter whose float reached the hot spot (under the tree) first, only one of them – mine – was going to disappear. The fact that this happened didn't surprise me at all though I was slightly disappointed that the perch responsible only weighed a pound. A menacing atmosphere began to descend on the river as we all cast again and I continued to make brazen predictions. Once again my float was the only one to submerge, but again it was only a modest fish. The curious fact is that we were all fishing the same way, presenting the bait at the same level with the same kind of tackle. The floats plopped simultaneously into the water and once more the race was on – with the same unseemly result, although this time I was lucky not to be thrown in as the perch was much bigger. I would certainly have been dunked had I cast a fourth time, but I wisely withdrew, gathered more kindling and made another pot of tea. There was a pause in proceedings as I passed round the cups again. Then out went the floats once more and the day ended with a satisfactory flourish, everyone landing beautiful, colourful perch.

Perch and tea. Perhaps if I had another cast now I might stop thinking about tea and return to my more serious addiction.

TWELFTH
CAST

The
Seasons
of an
Angler

The obvious temptation now, after I've spent the last hour or so taking dictation from the river, is to cast again and try for another perch. Like any other angler who's just made a catch, I'm always fairly eager to get my line back in the water, but if I've just landed something special I feel it's not only dishonourable to the fish but also to the occasion if I don't pause to properly appreciate the moment. For now, I still feel a three-pounder is just too glorious to share the day with anyfish else, and I don't care that, perch being shoal fish, there may be a strong possibility of an even bigger one. I have several angling friends who have made net-splitting hauls of huge perch, but if I caught a second sensation I feel it would probably take the gloss from the first. However, if I landed half a dozen and they were all huge, wouldn't that make this pleasant day yet more pleasant? Probably not, because each newly caught fish would diminish the worth, the special qualities, of the one before, reducing the original marvel to a unit in a row of numbers, like a sole lost in a shoal or a cod in a pod. I don't need a barrowful; all I ever hope is that, every now and then, some brilliant creature rises out of the secrecy of its river so I can rejoice in it and make a definite you-*are*-real-after-all contact.

If I was going to eat my catch I'd like to bring home more than one fish. Organically grown perch from a (reasonably) pure river are superior to trout, but, unfortunately for my family, I have raised them beyond the height of the kitchen table to the same status as the holy cow.

A fishing day without fish can never be a disaster or even just disappointing for there will always be something along the river to brighten the spirits. Yet though I can ruminate for hours on the look of the water or the reflection of the sky, it matters very much that I try my best to catch something. Furthermore, it must be the right kind of something. So if I hook a fish at this time of the year, at this particular season of my angling life, I'd prefer it to have stripes.

The perch is as emblematic of autumn as an amber leaf, a field of mist, a russet apple or a plume of bonfire smoke. It is the colour, charm and soul of an autumn river made fish-shaped. When I was a child, my first success was with summer fish from the village pond, but the first perch from a river was taken in the autumn, and it was so bright and boldly patterned that it made its still-water cousins seem drab and pasty in comparison and ever since then I've always associated proper perch fishing with autumn and rivers. I didn't catch a rod-bending perch for years, and apart from one dramatic episode never really cared, because whether from a pond or a river, small perch were nearly always eager for the bait and, above all else, a fisherboy has to constantly remind himself that he *can* catch fish. I think it's because my angling apprenticeship was served in the modest company of small perch that I'm now so impressed by the aristocracy. Not only does a big specimen of *Perca fluviatilis* look magnificent, it seems almost another kind of fish after those long seasons of six-inch tiddlers. Perch up to a pound may have a jaunty buccaneering appearance, but in shape they are entirely different to a fully formed adult, their outline being more fluid and curved, with transparent fins and round innocent eyes. A large perch on the other hand is more angular and muscular with a distinctive humped back, broad shoulders, powerful fins and a fierce, all-consuming, I've-got-your-number stare.

As a young angler I fished for little perch, I hoped for big perch, I once saw an immense perch, but mostly I dreamed about carp. Carp were the fish that sparked the angling gene in me and so, after I'd learned the basics of fishing lore from the schools of striped juveniles, I began an obsessive thirty-year season in pursuit of the giant goldfish. It was a tremendous adventure, and though I shall continue to enjoy midsummer jaunts to familiar and unfamiliar carp ponds – and no doubt continue to lose my sanity whenever a bow wave heads towards the far horizon – that season is really now over.

I suppose my fascination with carp first began to waver shortly after I'd caught the monster I always used to dream about. I had never fished exclusively for a leviathan, regarding such an ambitious project as not only futile but also misguided. For most of the time the dream was sufficient, but when the dream came true I couldn't dream it anymore – so when a pal introduced me to barbel fishing I was instantly converted. Within a few years I had moved house seventy miles westwards, away from a carp fisher's paradise – all lily-covered lakes and dark tree-hung pools – and into a barbel fisher's heaven – all swift-running streams and gin-clear water. And so a new season began, like a love affair, the flame in my head changing shape from the bold outline of *Cyprinus carpio* to the elegant form of *Barbus barbus*. The infatuation lasted twenty years and I still regard the barbel as a prince of the rivers – stately, aloof and mysterious, dominating a pool with its presence one day, vaporizing into rumour the next. You don't have to be a fish head to appreciate the barbel's superb scimitar profile, its asymmetrical tail, its small neat scales, its wing-like pectorals, its Roman nose, its graceful casual body language that is never argued with, even by the most ferocious current.

I remember reading once that a barbel is a poor man's salmon, but having had experience of both, I would say that a salmon is a poor man's barbel. A salmon has an epic life cycle and the dynamism of a bullet, while the barbel, though capable of jumping a weir, never migrates further than a few miles up- or downstream. However *Barbus* not only has more character than *Salmo salar*, its dynamism is that of the river itself – forceful, enduring but mercurial. It's always slightly disheartening to cast for one particular species and hook another, but I was never so dismayed as when I was fishing for barbel and a salmon grabbed my bait. However, like everyone else, I'm concerned and depressed by the fact that, over the last twenty years, the salmon has become almost as rare as a seahorse on our southern rivers. Although I recently had plans to explore every barbel river in the world, nowadays I find myself just too easily distracted by any water I come across that smells of perch.

Tench are another species that have long fascinated me – lovely, secretive fish that inhabit lily-covered lakes, slow rivers (there are tench in the quieter reaches of this stream), neglected canals and old reedy gravel pits. I especially like them because they are a summer fish and I can therefore sink deep into the meditative haze of the tench angler at a time when perch are not prickling my imagination. And because I don't find tench fishing as intense or as challenging as carp or barbel angling, its season will probably endure and continue to flower like a hardy annual until I'm too old to see my float.

In my teens I liked to think of myself as a chub expert, but the fish – which grew quite large on my local river – were really only a substitute for carp after the mini ice age of '62–63 had wiped out almost all piscean life in my local ponds. Chub fishing is now something I rarely get involved in, though last March I had a great day on this stretch of river, setting out merely with the idea of catching a few different species and ending up with two biggish roach and half a dozen superb, brassy, burly chub. I counted it as one of the best days of the season.

Roach have always been an occasional diversion, never a passion, though I suppose I did once lose my heart to a wonderful creature I saw ghosting across a pool on a little Suffolk river. I never caught it, but I still sometimes see it, drifting round the edge of some other kind of dream. Roach are a bit like perch in that you can catch lots of finger-sized fish and then see a monster of two pounds that makes your eyes spin – though it's always someone else who catches it.

I can see myself, in later years, adopting the rare and very subtle crucian carp as my summer passion and maybe turning to grayling through the winter. Crucians are very fastidious fish and they also seem to inhabit a different dimension from everything else, living invisibly in undisturbed ponds until a moment of harmonic convergence when your float moves a quarter of an inch. They are handsome, beautifully coloured, and when I land a big one (anything over one pound twelve ounces is big) it always lies placidly in the net and never loses its composure, as serene and dignified as a small bronze Buddha. (I count myself very fortunate to know a good man who spent a lifetime preserving the species and its habitat when most of Britain's crucians have been hybridized by feral goldfish.)

Grayling are as serene as crucians, but in a different way, being creatures whose exquisite lines evolved through millennia of fast currents and cold clear water. They look fragile and preciously elegant, but they are as tough as nails, will feed when the river is fringed in ice and, on the right tackle, fight as doggedly as barbel. They're probably the most beautifully coloured of all our freshwater fish, their silver flanks tinged with mauve and pale green and their sail-like dorsals flaring with the whole spectrum.

Though it may happen one day, I have yet to become wild about trout. Despite the fact that two of my favourite fishing books concern them, they are as a species not in the same league as those aforementioned. I could certainly never get wound up about still-water trouting. Someone once took me out in a gale in a boat on a vast concrete-lined reservoir, fishing for toy rainbow trout with gaudy-coloured leaded flies – an experience that would've delighted a frustrated mackerel fisher. However, proper trout fishing with a fly rod on a small wild river is a worthwhile occupation, especially as the best of it happens during the months that must always be out of bounds to the angler of spring-spawning fish. The trout spawn in winter and the season begins in April; therefore, while I see the swallows leaving today, the trout angler will see them coming back again next year. And instead of seeing the river darken and the trees become skeletal, the trout angler sees the water brightening and the green spreading like a flame from the reeds to the top of the willows.

THIRTEENTH
CAST

Let
There
Be
Gods

By remaining in the same place for long enough, I've noticed how the changing light has gradually reshaped the river. I suppose it must be about mid-afternoon – maybe four o'clock – and despite the continuing cloud cover, the sky is now markedly brighter to the west, which in turn is giving more definition to the ripples, creating an almost black and white diagram of the surface flow, with the variations of speed and direction clearly indicated. Furthermore, because of the contrast between reflected trees and reflected sky, the river appears to have broadened with new areas of detail visible along both banks.

Something else has changed: my intentions. The more I look at the water the more I realize that one biggish perch cannot, after all, suffice. Had I gone home an hour ago, I would've been more than happy, but because I stayed, the river has persuaded me that it's just absurd to sit by this good-looking pool for so long without making another cast. I have fed a few chopped worms into the swim and, no doubt, the minnows will now be frantically pecking at them. Individually, minnows look so harmless and goggle-eyed, but throw a shoal a worm and they become like tiny piranhas, tearing it to pieces in minutes. I don't mind if the minnows snaffle everything I offer; if there are perch in the vicinity, they'll quickly converge on the busy tiddlers and, once aroused, should be more interested in my bait.

Despite the two falls of rain – the first much heavier than the second – the water is as transparent as it looked this morning and just as slow-flowing, yet the smell of rain is still in the air and maybe the cumulative effect of several damp hours will work in my favour. So now I shall take up my rod again . . .

★

An hour – no, possibly half an hour – has passed and nothing much has happened except that I nearly lost my favourite float. A minute ago just after I missed a snatchy suspected chub bite, I cast again and got hooked up on some root or stone on the bottom and was forced to pull for a break. As the line snapped, the float zipped back into the air. I thought it was still attached, but it had flicked off the broken end and, the next moment, was floating free. I almost fell in as I tried to retrieve it, just reaching it with a net before it drifted under the tree. So, having re-tackled, I'm now letting the afternoon recover its calm for a moment before I try again . . .

If the changing light and the thinning cloud had altered the look of the river, something just happened to change its atmosphere. Half a dozen casts after I'd retied my line, I noticed a single minnow flip into the air down by the tree. There was no accompanying swirl to make me believe something was pursuing it. My quill sailed downstream and was almost at the same spot when it went *dib-dib-dibb* and vanished. Not a big fish, I told myself when I struck, but a perch all the same: the angular jagging made it obvious. It didn't take any line, and after a couple of deep dives conceded without any more fuss. The float reappeared through the surface and a moment later I could see a greenish back coming steadily towards me. About a pound, I thought. But then another movement caught my eye, just below and beyond my fish. Instantly, my heart sank as I thought it must be the pike again coming over to investigate a possible mouthful; but as it approached I saw that the shape was wrong. It rose a few inches higher in the depths, revealing the magical insignia – an array of very wide-apart black bands.

For a terrible, wonderful moment, I was convinced that the monster was going to grab hold of the lesser being. It wouldn't have been the first time I'd witnessed perch cannibalism on the end of my line, but surely my fish – at around twelve inches – was too much of a jawful. As the grandee came within a fin's-width of its potential prey, I stopped reeling and the river seemed to stop flowing. I prepared for a violent attack – which didn't occur. The monster may have been sizing the smaller fish up for its supper, or it may simply have been inquisitive, but after a superbly dramatic pause it turned away and with one sweep of the tail, bristled back into its sanctuary.

For a minute I just stared downstream and thought: was that or was that not the biggest perch I have ever seen? Then something jagged my elbow as the fish on the line started to tug again. I could almost hear it saying, 'Oi! What about me?' I apologized and quickly drew it in, releasing it without a second glance (though I do remember that it arrowed away upstream rather than down). Then I nervously re-baited with two of the biggest worms in my tin and cast out again, honestly believing I'd hook the monster in seconds. My confidence was wondrous; my disappointment, when, after a dozen or so casts, nothing had happened, was laughable.

Nothing happened. My casting became mechanical, then clumsy, but I kept on until I realized I was spoiling any chance I might have had. So now I've put my rod down and will give the pool a bit of a rest. It's probably about an hour till sunset, and last light is often the peak perch time. I might've thought of a better method by then.

This is obviously the best perch pool in the river –

though the more I think about the giant, the more I'm convinced it wasn't – as I first suspected – the same monster that Jason landed last season. Now the encounter has assumed an almost rational perspective, I guess it was probably a biggish four-pounder, which is still a whale of a perch. I think it was the manner of its entrance that made it look so astounding, especially after the last few uneventful hours. When it loomed up out of the depths it looked like some kind of river god. It *was* a river god. Now the pastoral tranquillity of this scene will always be completely at odds with its secret, which might not be revealed again.

FOURTEENTH
CAST

*Aqua
Lunar*

The cloud layer is still intact, though it looks as thin as paper over in the west where a low sun shines palely through. I don't think the sky will clear completely before dark; therefore I won't be able to enjoy the spectacle I was looking forward to. The moon is two days from full, which means it will be rising any moment now and would've looked good coming up from behind the hills to the east. Also, I had this idea that, as I don't have to hurry home to make supper, I could've fished on into the dark with the reflected moonlight making my float a clear silhouette. Fishing in moonlight, whether on still or running water, is always a delight, yet now I think about it, the tree's shadow would've limited my range, so float fishing would probably not have worked anyway.

A full September moon – when it's visible – is always an impressive sight, simply because it's so much more dominant than the preceding summer moons, which ride a much lower arc in the southern sky. The October moon will be higher again and so, though the evenings are closing in, the periods of brighter moonlight must affect the feeding times of a big-eyed fish like the perch. However, whenever the subject of fishing in moonlight is discussed, even though most anglers hardly ever remain on the river after dark, there seems to be a general pessimism, the consensus being that a bright moon usually puts the fish down. But I've landed some great fish in moonlight and one of the best catches of barbel I ever had was under a brilliant January moon when the fish were clearly visible whenever they rolled on the surface and I could even see the little silver ripple that my line made in the water. I haven't made enough nocturnal casts for perch to form an opinion about their lunar preferences, though, as with any debate about a particular kind of condition, there are always other factors to consider: temperature, wind, air pressure, clarity of water and whether you've still got any drinkable tea left in your flask.

I remember once meeting an angler who, rather than being keen on a particular species, or obsessed by a personal Moby Dick, was in thrall to the moon. He wasn't in the slightest bit romantic about it – his was a scientific passion. He was convinced that every single moment of a fishing day was not so much influenced as governed by the moon. He earnestly informed me that, if I was to give him the date and times of my next fishing trip, from the exact minute of my arrival on the bankside to my eventual departure, he would consult his tables of lunar phases and predict precisely my optimum pools of opportunity. Yet though I was impressed by the devotion he gave to his study, I politely declined his offer. I said I understood that, if the moon can heave an ocean halfway up a cliff, it can obviously cause a measurable shift in the waters of a river or lake. It must also subtly affect the buoyancy of a fish; but only a true lunatic would calculate his every cast according to the influence of its gravity.

Fishing in moonlight shouldn't, anyway, have to be reduced to an exercise in scientific theory; it should be more an appreciation of mysterious scene shifting; and if a fish gleams into view, let it be regarded only as a needle to stitch the magic together.

Around this time last year, I went fishing on the evening of a full moon, and became so absorbed in the river that, when the moon finally appeared, I didn't recognize it.

I arrived at the waterside an hour or two before sunset, thinking that although I might get an early chance of a fish, the perch would probably begin to feed in earnest at dusk. There was more strength in the current than today, but the river was still clinging to most of its summer growth. I fished my way down-stream, getting a small – a very small – fish on my second cast and then, after I'd tried several reedy pools and weedy glides, hooking and losing a much bigger one. My nose twitched when I was walking along a bit of high bank towards a usually productive pool. I hesitated a moment, then flipped out the bait.

The sun was setting; every colour was smudging

towards blue or gold while the river seemed to be softening from liquid to velvet.

The high bank made for awkward fishing, mainly because I had to keep low to stop myself being sky-lined. There were too many reeds to effectively use a float, so I just fished freeline, letting the worm drift into the narrow clear channels. Being up above the bankside vegetation, however, meant I had a better view of my surroundings, which was why I became aware of a dull amber dome beyond the eastern tree-line. For a moment, I couldn't understand what I was looking at. The colour was so deep and the object seemed so close that it couldn't have been anything other than an anchored hot air balloon or a weird circus-sized tent. Then I refocused properly and as it rose gradually out of the trees I wondered for the umpteenth time why proximity to the horizon should make the moon appear much larger than when it's high overhead. It was that heavy lustreless colour that, for a moment, convinced me it was earthbound. As it rose the amber brightened into gold, then pearl, then a radiant white that created a whole new world of shadows.

Something snicked at the line and made me jump, which was comic because first I'd been so intent on the fishing I hadn't recognized the moon, then I'd become so glued to the moon I'd almost forgotten I was still holding the rod. I struck and reeled in a fabulous gudgeon that must have weighed all of two ounces. He glinted at me in the moonglow and I could even see the speckles on his silver sides. Having plopped him back, I went down to the broader, more open pool that I'd intended to fish in the first place. I'd not long cast into it, however, when I felt a cold, chilling movement of air and within a few minutes a river mist began to form. All the brittle silhouettes of reeds and overhanging trees thinned into ghosts, and as the mist thickened, spilling over the banks, I almost lost sight of the water altogether. Only the vague reflection of the moon kept it in view.

I'm sure it wasn't because of the moon that I didn't get any more chances. Water may take much longer to cool than air, but if the process begins abruptly – and it was a very sudden chill – the cold-blooded fish usually respond in a cold-shouldering manner.

My hands became numb and I could feel the evening

crawling down my back. Not having dressed properly for the occasion, I soon realized that unless I quickly got bored with the fishing I would surely die. Also, it once happened, after I fished too long on a night of dense mist, that I got hopelessly lost simply trying to cross an open field, ending up going round in impossible circles and twice almost falling in. But last September was different because, when I finally walked away from the river, the moon was looking down over the head-high fog, guiding me safely home.

FIFTEENTH
CAST

———— ❧ ————

The
Church
of the
Perch

S till no break in the cloud, though the western half of the sky remains reasonably bright. After the middle of September the evenings draw in quickly, yet, at the moment, time seems to have slowed down again, allowing me to make dozens more futile offerings to the god under the alder tree. But he is not impressed. Even though I have sacrificed a minnow in his name, he denies me, for I am not worthy. Now I have taken the float from the line and flicked out the bait so that it rolls right under the overhanging branches, following it up with a handful of chopped worms. The rod is lying across the vegetation; the reel has its check switched on and I shall wait for it to sing to me while I let this other line – this pen line – run on to the moment when I can't see it anymore. If nothing further happens I know that I'll always be drawn back to this spot, despite the fact that the perch may soon decide to avoid it. Today the pool is its sanctuary, its lair, its perfect refuge, but if it doesn't pounce on my bait in the next half-hour I'll inevitably spend many more days fishing here, unperturbed by the fact that it may have gone elsewhere.

At least, as this bit of river is fairly inaccessible and doesn't have much of a local reputation, it should remain largely undisturbed, but there is always the danger that, once a great fish has established a new church, word will spread and pilgrims will gather and turn the fishing into an organized religion. I can think of dozens of places where either a tremendous catch or a glimpsed monster transformed an ordinary stretch of water into somewhere worshipful, where, if I wanted to fish, I would have to bow my head and join a queue. So, from now on, this pool is on a river in Ireland.

There was a deep pool in the first river I ever

fished where, among the sunken lilies, I once saw an enormous chub – perhaps an eight-pounder. It turned me into a fanatic and for several seasons I was a permanent fixture on the overgrown bank, always hoping that I'd be lucky one day and not only see the fish again but also tempt it. And one morning, during my second season, I had my opportunity: the giant suddenly reappeared, took my bait confidently and in a single unbelievable lunge shredded a whole lily bed, my nerves and my line. However, all my waiting for him to reappear wasn't in vain, because I learned how to read a river, and I also caught dozens of lesser chub, though nearly all of them were proper rod-benders.

Unfortunately, I made the mistake of revealing my secret to a famous specimen hunter and afterwards the pool was never the same again. Once he'd seen the swim's potential for himself he believed, or at least partially believed, my stories. And, because he began very visibly fishing there, rumours circulated and other anglers started to appear. At the end of the season the place looked worn out, and of course the fish had all disappeared. It would be interesting to see what it's like now, nearly forty years later. Hopefully it's become neglected and forgotten again – just as I had to forget about it when the pilgrims came.

Yet who am I to complain? I'm as guilty as any other angler of eagerly following up a rumour and chasing down someone else's vision. The very reason I'm fishing this stretch of river is because Jason foolishly made some remark about a big fish when we met as strangers, crashing our shopping trolleys together by the fresh-fish stand in a local supermarket. (Like me he's a single father and he has three young boys to look after. What does this say about angling and marriage?)

When I was young – long before I saw that big chub – it didn't matter that most of the big fish stories I heard were either exaggerations or complete fantasies. I wanted to believe in the myth of the giant carp that lived in a municipal boating pond because then I'd have the courage to fish there after dark when the park gates were locked. Knowing the history of the fabled leviathan that lived under the bridge, where my friends and I fished for gudgeon, lent drama and gravitas to something that otherwise might've seemed like just another childhood game. But to become too attached to one specific place, to become too devout a worshipper of one particular god, can lead to a kind of madness – a lesson I learnt back at my village pond when I was twelve.

Dave, Mick and I had something of a competition going, each trying to be the first to catch six fish by teatime. We'd all caught one or two, but before anyone neared the magic half-dozen, two unknown grown-up fishermen appeared. Their great creels, well-stuffed rod holdalls and clumping thigh waders – which we had never seen before – impressed us immediately. They trudged round the pond, heading directly, without a sideways glance at us or anyone else, towards an unfishable spot on the far bank.

It was rare for such obviously experienced and well-equipped anglers to descend on our small paradise, but it was also intriguing that they should choose to fish by the boggy reed bed where there was nowhere to sit and read comics when the fish weren't biting. Despite our competition, we reeled in and wandered over to watch the masters at work, though naturally we kept our distance and feigned boredom. Their rods were twice as long and far more delicate than ours – maybe fourteen- or fifteen-footers, Spanish reed probably, with whiskery split-cane tips. Once they were ready to fish they produced a large biscuit tin almost overflowing with a bait we knew only by repute: maggots. Having tipped the grubs into canvas shoulder bags they waded beyond the marginal reed bed and stood in the open water where the depth would have been too much for our wellingtons. They cast out their floats, sprinkled handfuls of the lovely-looking larvae around them and stood silently like two patient herons.

Though I'd only been fishing for two seasons, I had correctly deduced that a float poised on the surface was the most attractive and tantalizing sight in fishing, even when it was not my own. Particularly as these blokes seemed to know exactly what they were doing, there was an extra voltage in the charged stillness of their quills. We could have watched them for the rest of the afternoon and were disappointed that, because we were having a whispered argument about something, we didn't actually witness the first moment of dematerialization. There was a kind of jump in the corner of our eyes and we turned to see the angler on the right reeling in an average-sized perch. He unhooked it, flicked it back in the water with a dismissive gesture, re-baited and re-cast. A short while later they both caught small perch almost simultaneously and, wondering what all the fuss was about, we shrugged our shoulders and began to walk back to our own rods.

Halfway round the pond we heard an unusual sound – the staccato rasping of a reel. No one in our history had ever hooked a fish that pulled line off the reel. We looked back and saw one of the rods curving and jabbing, the tip pointing down at a small explosion of spray and ripples. With our boots thumping on the hard clay bank, we raced back and arrived by the reeds just in time to see the angler on the left lean forward with a landing net and calmly enmesh a huge fish for his companion.

'What is it?!' we shouted.

There was a bit of a flurry and then the angler lifted the miracle up to show us.

'Whoar!' we sang.

We knew about the carp – after all, I'd seen them – but we had never imagined that the pond held a perch as big as a carp. It was pale yellow, with amber fins, indistinct dark stripes, and it took *two hands* to hold. For quite a long time after the fish was returned, we couldn't quite believe what we'd seen.

We went back to our rods, but we didn't finish the match; I don't think we even re-cast. We just babbled endlessly about a fish that was like the discovery of a new species and an obscure corner of the pond that was like the discovery of America.

Leaving the two heroic anglers still fishing, we went home to hatch a plan that would secure permanent rights to the reed bed; and early next morning, before anyone else appeared on the pond, we made a big platform of branches in the reeds so we could stand without getting a bootful and cast into the hallowed square yard of water. There was enough space for the three of us and the contents of our bags, which included the usual picnic and bottle of Tizer, a tin of worms, a pencil case full of floats and hooks, our comics and, for reference only, *The Observer's Book of Freshwater Fishes*. As well as detailing all the biological essentials, the book offered instructions on fishing. However, in the perch section, the technical descriptions were too convoluted for us to follow; also the book seemed to be ambivalent about baits, advising us to offer both a maggot and a worm on the complex, double-hooked rig. After due consideration we decided to stick with the worm.

The first casts were throat-dryingly dramatic, and the first dip of the float was, after all the anticipation, too much of a real thing. We botched our first strikes by reacting too nervously, but then we calmed down and began to catch some fish, a few perch of the size we could catch anywhere else on the pond. However, the water in front of us was unlike anywhere else on the pond and, all day, our faith in it never wavered and the little perch we pulled out of it could not diminish its magic. Of course we knew we weren't quite equal to it: our tackle was inferior, our worms had been dug from the compost heap and we didn't have a landing net. But our main concern was that we had no idea what would happen if, terrifyingly, a float went down and stayed down. The fear of that just-possible reality kept us unusually quiet until evening.

It was August, summer holidays, and we therefore had an eternity to fish the monster spot and outwit, or outwait, a dragon-sized perch. We hadn't succeeded on the first day because we hadn't used the right bait, so on the second day we called in at the village corn stores and asked if they sold maggots. Unfortunately they did not, nor could they tell us where to find any. Seeing our disappointment, and not wanting us to go away empty-handed, the woman behind the counter offered us some Spratts Angler's Bait – a brownish paste that came in a little plastic tub and smelled of shoe polish. Maybe it *was* shoe polish. We politely refused it, but before we went back to the pond, I noticed the booklets on the counter: Ditchfield's Little Wonder Books. Amongst *Popular Pets*, *How to Grow Your Own Vegetables* and *Keeping Ducks and Geese* was *Fishing for All Ages*. Flicking through it, I came to the section on perch ('the most handsome of all') and read aloud the line: 'He will take all kinds of bait, *but a worm is the best.*'

Our confidence restored, we once more took possession of the boggy reed bed and, with the best bait in the world, spent another day within casting distance of the biggest perch in the world. We realized there was every possibility that the monster would occasionally roam round the rest of the pond, but we felt certain that the two master anglers had, perhaps accidentally, discovered his secret feeding area. For maybe four or five more days we continued our wonderful quest – and then, suddenly, we gave up, exhausted, accepting that the monster's presence and our close proximity to it was all we could ask. To have continued would have made us as mad as Captain Ahab.

We had caught lots of unexceptional perch, at least a dozen gudgeon and one small but remarkable rudd. We had fished ourselves into a strange trance in which nothing, not even the catapults of the rodless infidels, could hurt us or deflect us from our cause. For almost a week I had gone to bed each night with the water still rippling behind my closed eyes and my float like a candle in the middle of my dreams. Dave, likewise, felt his bed was floating, and though Mick said he just slept like a stone, each morning we were, all three, equally wild about getting back to the pond. We didn't, however, learn any new techniques or try any novel baits or use any different tackle or change our methods. We had lost the will to improvize. Nothing sensational happened, but our fishing had never seemed so complete.

SIXTEENTH
CAST

*The
Dreamline*

I am sitting in the kitchen in Jason's cottage, having just walked back through the luminous dark. The last hour before I packed up was quite intense as fish began to splash and swirl all along the length of river, though I think they were mostly chub and dace. As soon as I began losing sight of the rod, lying next to me, I picked it up and felt for bites – something that, in the dark, is even more tantalizing than watching a float, especially when you've just seen the fish of your dreams. Three times the line was snicked – but not by fish. There was a quick tightening, but on each occasion, just as I was about to react, I either saw or heard a bat fluttering past the rod point. This is a common complaint of the night fisher, a consequence of the super-sensitive insectivore pinpointing the line with its radar and confusing it with a midge. The line remained untrembled by anything below the surface and finally I accepted the monster's truce. I reeled in, bundled up my stuff and headed back downstream, everything clearly visible in the cloud-diffused moonlight (I never carry a torch at night as it only limits the view).

Tawny owls called, a heron shouted at me when I disturbed it on the shallows, a pair of ducks, horrified by my passing silhouette, smashed out of a still pool and I thought I heard the whistle of an otter. Finally, the path led me away from the water, and after just a few yards it seemed as if the night had stopped breathing and the river had sunk underground.

Five minutes further on, over the fields and along a dark tree-hung track, I came to this bright kitchen, where Jason is about to pour me a mug of tea. His eldest son, Robin, has been showing me the model of a pirate ship that he's just made, his two other boys are wondering what I'm writing about, unable to make any sense of my messy scrawl, and the day ends happily with the clink of heavy China and a plume of fragrant steam.

Now it's the next morning, Friday, and the weather has kept the promises it was making yesterday. I'm at home, trying to avoid an article I'm meant to be writing, and the light beyond my window is grey and washed out. The rain came in the night, like an army charging across the roof. The roar of it woke me in the small hours and, despite our desperate need of it, I could only think glumly about the leaking gutters and how a whole dry summer had passed without me even trying to mend them. But then reason came to my aid, making the perfectly valid point that there was never time to mend them. The whole point about being a crazed angler is that there can never be 'spare time' to attend to domestic chores. An angler doesn't need an excuse for neglecting such things as gutters, exterior paintwork and lawns; in fact he should only feel guilty if something unavoidable happens to make him miss a prime angling opportunity. Chores can always be stored up for the close season, although for me this is spring, when it's necessary to visit every wood and wild place in the area to confirm that the world is still working and that all the migrants – especially the nightingales – have returned.

The rain continued to hammer, telling me that I am just lazy, that despite being a fish head I spend much more time at home than on the river; therefore I have no excuses for idling. If I'm lucky I might fish twice a week but rarely for an entire day, and hardly ever at weekends – though it would be different if I didn't have my children to love. The rain finally made me promise that, just for my children's sake, I must fix the gutters before winter, and as the storm died back to no more than a steady drizzle, I drifted away and was immediately fishing again.

I was on a deep clear river that zigzagged through flat open country. A friend said he'd had a great catch of chub from a side stream not far from where I was fishing, so I went to have a look. The stream was almost as wide as the main river, and the current nearly as strong, but it slowed at a sharp right-angled bend. I cast my float just below the bend, lost sight of it and realized I'd hooked a fish – quite a good fish. It raced off upstream and, as I hurried after it, my reel came loose and fell off the rod handle. I continued running, holding the line and trying to keep it clear of the bankside bushes. There were some boys playing in the field behind me and I asked them to come and help, and eventually we got the reel back on the rod. However, I'd allowed myself to step too far away from the stream, and when I wound up the slack I realized the line had caught in the topmost branches of several tall trees. Despite my efforts to unravel the tangle, the day ended before I could reel myself back to the fish.

As I walked back across the fields, I kept the rod high and allowed the line to run freely from the reel so that the next morning I could wind myself back to wherever the fish had gone. Still trailing line, I entered the town where I was staying, passing between houses and along busy streets, weaving through crowds of people who had come to watch some annual event. Some of the boys were still walking along with me, excited about what had happened, and I met them again the next morning, when I followed the line over a bridge onto the other side of the river downstream of the town. Incredibly, it was still unbroken and I began rewinding it, trying to feel if there was anything alive still attached to the end. I reeled myself back upstream, over a different bridge and along a path crowded with people expectantly waiting, on and on until the day was almost over and I was miles from where I'd first made contact. Finally, the line led me to another side stream, much narrower and faster-flowing than the first, where the rod tip suddenly pointed down to a little reed bed under the bank.

Yes, there was definitely something there, but I couldn't ease it into open water. I sat down on the bank, took off my shoes and socks and prepared to go in for it. Maybe it wasn't a big chub after all; I had a strong suspicion it might be a sea trout.

Even when I'm sleeping I'm still fishing, though my watery reveries will soon be washed aside. The clock stands at half past three. In a moment my forty-eight hours of solitude will end and I'll be swept away again on the ever-rolling stream of fatherhood . . .

Here they come.

'I've learnt to juggle!' says Alex.

'I've been invited to a party!' says Ellen.

'Come and hear my new tune!' says Will.

(Camilla is at university, so I can't report on what she might be saying.)

I'd like to tell them about my big perch and the apparition that came to look at me, but they've heard these kinds of stories too many times before and, at the moment, there are more urgent things for them to attend to – like practising juggling ('Can I use these oranges?') or playing the guitar.

All my children have enjoyed fishing: Camilla was a brilliant angler when she was a junior and Ellen caught her first fish when she was an infant; Alex stalks carp like a cat and Will recently showed us all how to catch bass in the sea. But because fishing has always been such a background to their lives it's not special enough at present to distract them from riding motorbikes in the woods, forming a band of musicians or going to parties and meeting new friends. Every summer we spend a few days fishing together and something lovely or dramatic always happens. But I think only one of my children will continue in the family tradition. While the others talk of different kinds of dreams, Will often says he wants to go back to the lake where he once saw a giant carp.

But it's probably best that I don't tell anyone, not even my children or my most trusted friends, about the great perch. If I remain silent, at least for a while, it might still be there when I go back to the river.

SEVENTEENTH
CAST

*The
Well
in My
Garden*

My well was hand-dug through seventy feet of solid chalk in the mid-eighteenth century. Two men worked with pick, shovel and bucket – one down below, one on the surface – until they reached the watercourse which they – or their trusty dowser – knew was flowing below them. According to local records, the well only failed twice in the whole of the twentieth century – in 1911 and 1976. I feel, however, that it may fail more regularly this century and, despite the rain of the last twenty-four hours, it is dry now, though of course the water will eventually percolate through. My last cottage, which was on greensand rather than chalk, had a sweet-watered well that never failed, whatever the season, but now I'm quite glad that this house is on the mains. Last summer and the summer before, the well only had a few inches of water in it, though in the winter of 2000 the level rose almost fifty feet.

Health and Safety must regard wells – there are hundreds in this area – as a special hazard, and they no doubt have whole lists of regulations and guidelines warning of the dangers of falling in. If an inspector ever saw how I protect my kids from doing a ding-dong-bell they'd no doubt charge me with negligence. The well head consists of a low circular brick wall and there used to be half a wood door laid across it. But now there's just a plank with some potted plants, though this makes it much easier when John the well dipper comes to make his monthly check on the water level. The well is only a few feet from the front door, but in the twenty years I've been living here, no one, thankfully, has ever come even close to toppling in, though I would constantly remind my shoal of the potential. We have, however, dropped a fair level of pebbles and coins down into the long column of darkness and it's always a curious pleasure to remove the plank and stare down at the circular reflection of the sky deep, deep below.

The winterbournes round here usually start flowing just before Christmas and disappear again in early spring. Last year these winter-flowing streams only managed to dribble for a week, but in 1999 they rose in November and quickly became gushing torrents, continuing to gush until late April. At night, when it wasn't raining, I thought I could sometimes hear the water flooding through the fissures in the chalk and bubbling up in the fields at the bottom of the valley. The village pond rose so high that we had carp swimming down the street, much to the delight of Alex, who would chase them under the garden fences and hedges and catch them in his hands.

The underground stream upon which our well is situated eventually rises just beyond our neighbouring village, several miles away, and flows on as a clear shallow brook which is eventually joined by other streams until it's almost big enough to be called a river. Twelve miles from the well, this little river – which is home to trout, dace, otters and native crayfish – joins the larger river that I fished yesterday, and I'm some-how reassured, even comforted, by that physical con-nection. Since August, however, the drought has made this link seem tenuous, like a power cable with no live current, though soon the rain will recharge it again.

Several miles before the stream reaches the conflu-ence with the river its transparent water is suddenly spread out over six acres by a centuries-old stone dam, creating a lake that used to hold an enormous carp. In the few years I fished there I only saw this monster once and even then it wasn't a clear view; yet it appeared immense compared to the other carp I would occasionally see, none of which looked under twenty pounds. They were, however, very ancient creatures, maybe sixty years old, and, therefore, as several seasons have passed since I last fished there, maybe the big one is just bones in the lake bed now.

Being so old, the fish were also very wise, and though I could sometimes get them feeding over a scattering of corn they would invariably peck each individual grain until there was just one left. It was always the same one: the one on my hook. For several seasons they never made a mistake, but then, in the last summer, I got a twenty-two-pounder that I crept up on as it was feeding near the dam, then, a month later, a twenty-six-pounder that I first spotted in the rear-view mirror of my car.

It was the last day I ever fished at the lake and the conditions were perfect – sultry, thundery, with a warm intermittent rain. I was convinced the fish would be in a mood to let their scales down and was therefore amazed, after I had quietly stalked through all the usual feeding areas, that I didn't see so much as a fin. Even the little splashy trout weren't in evidence.

There's a track that runs along the lake's southern bank and I'd parked my car in the nettles halfway down towards the dam. As there was nothing happening – I like to stalk carp rather than sit and wait for them – and as the rain and thunder had suddenly intensified, I resigned myself to a castless final day. Stowing my rod and net in the back of the car, I reversed up to a gap in the bankside vegetation where I could turn round and head home, but as I swung into the clearing, checking my mirror to see I wasn't getting too close to the water's edge, I was taken (further) aback by the sight of a large tail waving at me. It was only there for a moment – then it was gone.

Had I imagined it? I turned round for a clearer look and after a while it reappeared, rising slowly above the surface like a black heart-shaped flag, ten yards from the bank. The carp it belonged to was feeding enthusiastically on something, tilting its tail up every time it nosed down in the relatively shallow margins.

Switching the engine off, I gathered up my tackle, slipped out of the car – making sure the door didn't make a click – and, keeping low, crawled to within casting distance. The rain had eased again to a steady drizzle and my first unobstructed view was fairly heart-stopping: not one but five big carp, like cattle at a trough, shoulder to broad shoulder, browsing on a heap of grain that the keeper must have thrown in to attract wild duck. The fish that kept flaunting its tail looked like a mid-twenty-pounder; there were three others a little smaller and one that looked to be over thirty pounds – deep-bodied and almost a yard long.

To cast corn to carp grazing on corn might have seemed like trying to catch a cow with a blade of grass, but their fodder was plain, mine was zingy with essence of mango. I was using an eight-foot stalking rod that Edward – the master can-splitter – had made me only the season before; the reel was a four-inch centre pin loaded with twelve-pound line, and I flicked out three grains on an unweighted size 6 barbless, landing the bait without a splash just in front of the biggest fish. However, I'd cast *over* a lesser fish, which drifted to one side with the line hitched across its back. I had a moment of panic as the line began to tighten, but I managed to flick it free and the fish seemed undisturbed.

The water was only two feet deep where the corn lay and so clear that, had it not been for the light rain on the surface, I would've been able to see the carp close its mouth over my bait. Through the myriad of tiny spreading rings, I watched the biggest fish turn and make way for its high-tailed companion, who nosed down with a slow decisiveness that any seasoned carp-stalker would have recognized. My line began to tighten and, being so close, I needed only to give the rod a little nudge to set the hook. There was a thunderous swirl that seemed to lift up half the lake. The sensation through the line and down the rod was of overwhelming power, and the reel made a sound like a chainsaw.

For a moment it was impossible to tell which bow wave was mine, but then I could see my line stretching behind the one about to enter the vast bed of mare's tail only thirty yards away. Increasing pressure, I swung the rod over, causing another upswirl on the edge of the sanctuary. The carp plunged, diving round in a tight half-circle, and things became a bit violent until I remembered to think calm, to ease rather than heave. The fish responded by swimming in wider, less frantic circles, and I gained a few yards each time it came round towards me, but lost them again when it swept away. The debate, however, was going my way and apart from one forceful argument about an overhanging tree on my left there were no more bitter disagreements. Finally, I waded out into the margin with my big landing net and the fish came rolling in almost lazily over the mesh.

In the water it had looked smoky grey, but on the bank, in the rain, it was a lovely glistening of cobalt blue, amber and gold. Its head was grooved and time-worn like the head of the Sphinx, and its round gold-rimmed eyes stared at me reproachfully until I lowered it, with apologies, back into the water and let it swim out of my arms and into the forest of weeds.

EIGHTEENTH
CAST

Confluence

When I looked down the well shaft this morning, three weeks after the deluge, I saw a luminous blue disc with a little black blob on one side of it. The blue was the sky and the blob was my head silhouetted against it. After all that time the water had finally filtered through and will now be flowing again along the subterranean channels, out into the valley, through the lake, over the dam, along the stream and down to the confluence with the river. At that point, however, it is utterly different to the narrow, winding upper reaches where I glimpsed the monster perch. The confluence stretch is broad, deep, straight and on the edge of a busy market town. There is a noisy, graffiti-scrawled road bridge; there are warehouses, schoolboys in boats, dog walkers and, even worse, an unacceptable number of other anglers, some of whom I count as friends and who deliberately arrive on the river early just so that they can get to the best perch holes before me. Hugh, for instance, always gets to the river before me and most of the time he's not even fishing for perch. But I must not be disrespectful because it was Hugh who first introduced me to this stretch and, in doing so, unwittingly changed the course of my fishing.

Since the 1980s I had been happily spending most of my autumns and winters in search of the increasingly huge and yet increasingly elusive barbel, but then, early in 2001, Hugh made a wonderful catch of big perch and phoned me to describe the stripes. At the time very few people fished the confluence stretch for perch and he invited me down there for a day in March, almost promising me a fish from his newly discovered secret swim. I was happy to accept as my favoured barbel river, a few miles east of here, hadn't produced anything since the previous November and

I was beginning to forget what a tight line felt like. Reacquainting myself with the pleasures of perch fishing was something I'd been vaguely considering for several seasons. I'd not deliberately set out to fish for perch or even accidentally caught a decent-sized specimen since I was a teenager. It wasn't just my carp and barbel obsession that had caused me to neglect them. During the '70s and '80s the species was almost wiped out by a mysterious disease, but as they recovered and rivers were recolonized, so stories of occasional huge fish began to circulate, prompting me to blow the dust from my old perch floats and once again dream perch-shaped dreams.

March 2001 began in characteristic fashion: cold and wild. Though the wind was less constant on the day I'd arranged to meet Hugh, it was still from the east, which in early March nearly always means mean. Hugh said that, apart from me, he'd told no one about his special swim other than an angling pal who had a tackle shop to manage and therefore would not be disturbing us. The chances of anyone else fishing the river on a cold, grey mid-week morning were slim and so Hugh said it wouldn't matter that I couldn't get to the bankside till 9 o'clock. Naturally, he'd be on the river slightly earlier.

On a normal school day the bus arrives at my house at 8.10 a.m., and in the half-hour that precedes that time, the tranquil atmosphere of our home is invariably transformed into a chaos of lost socks, lost homework, last-minute lunch boxes, suddenly remembered notes to teachers and final demands for the bathroom. The crisis builds to the wonderfully comic moment when a 'toot toot' signals the arrival of the bus and everyone begins to hop around the room putting their shoes on while simultaneously shouldering their school bags. And then, suddenly, the storm is over. The bus burbles off down the road with my unfortunate children, the front door closes and the kettle begins to steam. Even when I'm going fishing, the first cup of tea in that blissful calm has to be savoured very slowly. Because of this, and my usual habit of ignoring the clock on a fishing day, I was rather late meeting Hugh, not that this really mattered because the manager of the tackle shop had taken an unexpected day off, casting into the chosen swim at first light. It looked the perfect perch hideout: a big willow overhanging a slow bend, exactly as Hugh had described. I found him looking cold and a bit frustrated in a less attractive pool upstream.

'We should've come here yesterday,' he said.

Apparently the manager had landed nine fish already, up to two and a half pounds. Hugh had only had one, of about a pound, though he was confident that, having groundbaited the swim, larger fish would follow. He invited me to share the pool with him, saying I should fish the downstream end with the float, while he concentrated on the upper half with a ledger rod. The whole morning passed with hardly a flicker of response from the fish, but I didn't care because I was happy just watching my float. It was also a pleasure to be using a lighter, more sensitive rod than usual. Edward had made me a Stradivarius of float rods – twelve feet of finely crafted cane that would have been too delicate for barbel or carp but seemed ideal for perch. With the cold conditions and the water low and clear, Hugh had stressed the importance of fine tackle and so I was also fishing with a centre pin loaded with two-pound line, a slim, three-shot balsa float and a 14 hook baited with a single red maggot and a very small worm. Despite such delicacies, however, there was only one little dip of the float in four hours. Meanwhile, the manager, who was using a heavy, worm-stuffed feeder and a lob tail, had earned a few more penalty points by landing three more fish.

Lunch, said Hugh, would make all the difference. Washed down with Guinness and scalding tea, a bagful of sandwiches quickly restored our optimism. I took my rod and headed upstream, feeling so certain I'd find a more productive pool that I said that I'd be calling for the net in 'under seven minutes'. Meanwhile, Hugh dispensed with his perch gear and began to fish for his beloved roach.

Within the allotted time I'd found a nice deepish run that took my float round the roots of a tree where, straightaway, it dipped under and I hooked my first fish of the day. Typically, it wasn't a perch, but I still needed the net. Hugh seemed quite impressed, but then any roach will make him tremble. He'd just headed downstream when I cast again and had another, more hesitant, sliding sort of bite that didn't really convince until I tightened into a firm resistance. This is no roach, I told myself.

'Is it a pike?' asked Hugh, looking anxiously at the severe but static bend in the rod.

With such light tackle, I couldn't do more than tease the fish up to me, but after a minute or so the float reappeared, rising diagonally from the depths and eventually quivering in the air between rod tip and river. Soon we glimpsed a pale gold flank and then clearly saw the black barring. The fish finally rolled sploshing over the net, raising a happy cheer as I realized it had to be my best perch to date: two and three quarter pounds. In the dull afternoon light, lying amongst the dead, sepia-toned reeds, its colours looked impossible. Because I'd not caught a sizeable perch for almost thirty years, the moment was a bit like a meeting with a dear friend who I hadn't seen for all that time and yet who was somehow completely unchanged. The perch, however, just stared furiously at the untrustworthy world and, as soon as I lowered him back into the river, burst out of my hands and swept away under his tree.

Hugh returned to roach fishing, but I waited a while before casting again. A cold, sleety rain began to fall, but I didn't feel it. When it eased off a little, I got another beauty – two pounds, nine ounces – from exactly the same place by the tree roots. Then, with the rain slanting down more heavily through the bitter wind and the school bus probably halfway home, it was definitely time to go.

Driving back along the valley and up into the hills, I hummed a merry and mindless tune. It was good to be a perch fisher again.

NINETEENTH
CAST

Return

Having waited long enough for the river to settle after the deluge, I hurried back to the prime pool today – hardly pausing on my way along the bank to see what the water was looking like. The memory of my last visit was so strong it seemed to blind me to the present moment and I could only think about getting my line in the water and preparing for the biggest perch in the universe. But the river, which had been so friendly and forthcoming last week, was completely uncommunicative. In fact it was asleep.

Having cast out and allowed the float to drift down to the alder and settle beneath the branches, I gradually became aware of a stillness and a kind of sullenness over the water, as if a spell, not a float, had been cast. And I knew that, whatever ploy I tried, I was going to have an absolutely uneventful day.

The surface remained unbroken by any rising fish and even the minnows seemed to have migrated. Though the reeds and weeds had obviously been bashed about a bit in the spate, the water was now almost as transparent and just a little higher than before. The air temperature had certainly dipped after a few chilly nights, but I didn't think it was cool enough to put the fish down; rather I'd presumed it might encourage them to feed through the day. Obviously something else had affected them.

Had there been some filthy agricultural spillage somewhere upstream? It had happened before, ten years ago, with devastating results. Thankfully, I was sure this wasn't the case today because when I finally gave up, after about four soporific hours, and headed back downstream, I eventually discovered a shoal of minnows playing happily in the shallows – and minnows are very sensitive to bad stains in the water.

But where, last time, the whole landscape had

seemed to be re-energized by the onset of autumn, today it had decided to hibernate. I should have done the same.

TWENTIETH
CAST

The
Third
Day

When I arrived today, in mid-morning, it looked like a different river. Where before it had flowed low, slow and clear between the reed beds, now it was running high and powerfully, the colour of milky tea. Only the tips of the reeds were visible, bent and quivering like grass in a gale while most of the weeds and all the lilies had been swept away. After another period of dry weather there was heavy rain again last night, but I didn't think it would affect the river so quickly. Yet though it was rising I decided the colour wasn't too heavy to deter a wide-eyed perch.

I started to walk slowly upstream, enjoying all the

new things the river was talking about. At first it was gurgling, like the sound of cattle drinking, where it washed round underbank tree roots; then there was a heavier, rhythmic pounding, like the sound of a paddle steamer, where it pulsed and swirled over a fallen tree. The river sank into a whisper when I began walking away from the first bends and along the deep straight, but if I stopped and listened, I could hear it again, rippling and furling over those places where some change in the riverbed deflected or slowed the current.

Though there was an intermittently strong southerly breeze, the willows stood silent in it; all their foliage had gone in a week. The alders still had most of theirs but, probably because of a frost three nights ago, the leaves were more thin and papery than before; they hissed dryly in the wind. The rooks were talkative and seemed to be enjoying the conditions as they tumbled about over the edge of the woods, but the only other bird voices I heard were from a few passing redwings, the familiar flight call of the local kingfishers and – now and then – the robin's autumn lament. A sweeter sound, however, was the rising glissando of my taut line in the breeze as a big fish drove out into the main current and hunkered down in some old lily roots.

Arriving at my new favourite pool, I realized I couldn't fish it as before because the flow was coming in too swiftly round the high bank, and where there had been quiet deeps beneath the tree there was now a convulsion of upswirls, vortices and opposing currents. Disappointed, I half thought I'd head back downstream and look for a less turbulent spot, but the slack along the far bank caught my eye and I had a feeling that, as the conditions had only just altered, the local inhabitants might have just drifted over into temporary accommodation.

Holding my rod as high as possible to keep the line clear of the midstream flow, I let a large cork-bodied quill work its way slowly down the opposite bank. After only a dozen or so casts, the float dragged under and I was into a heavy fish. Of course I was thinking big perch, but after a wonderfully deceiving moment of perch-like stubbornness, the pressure changed and something swept up and then down and across, finally lodging in the underwater root system.

When I raised the tension, the breeze-blown line

sounded like a violin in its highest register. I was by then convinced I'd hooked a chub; fortunately, it came clear and I brought it safely upstream, though it made a bit of a splash in the strong underbank flow when I tried to persuade it over the net. It would – at four and a half pounds – have made a magnificent perch, but it was still quite a nice-looking chub, with bright silver flanks and a very blue tail. And, having caught it, I thought there'd be more fin room for the perch and also more time for them to make up their minds about worms.

The sun burst through the breaking cloud and, to add to my hopes, the river level seemed a fraction lower than when I arrived. I cast again – an overambitious swing that flew the tackle straight into the far reed bed. As soon as I tightened I knew I was going to lose the hook, but I got the float back. I was more careful next time and hooked another fish before the float had properly settled. This time I knew instantly it was a chub; the unhesitating dash downstream was like a clear signature. It was a three-pounder and, over the next hour, I followed it with two more similar-sized fish and one very pretty roach.

Although I was certain the perch were not in their church because of the storm surge pouring through the ever-open doors, if they were in the quiet backwater they weren't paying attention to the local availability of worms. Being intolerant of any other species not small enough to fit into their mouths, I guessed they had moved off to a more sheltered harbour, maybe a permanent wintering place where they would remain until next spring. However, while I might quickly relocate some of the shoal, it might not be so easy to find the monster again. Despite the tribal preferences of the majority, the big matriarchs usually live a more solitary existence, although I remember a fellow percologist, Jardine, telling me how, late in the summer, months after the spawning period, he discovered a shoal of huge fish – three- and four-pounders – lying together in a clear glide. What made the sighting particularly unique was the addition of a similar-sized pike loitering among the stripes. Perhaps it was just pretending to be a perch, or maybe it thought it was lying in a reed bed, but after a while the perch decided its presence was an offence against the laws of nature. Jardine watched as one of the shoal turned suddenly, grabbed the pike across its narrow shoulders and gave it a good shaking, holding it down hard on the riverbed as it did so. After a few violent seconds, the pike rolled away and lanced downstream while the vermin controller returned to the shoal.

For hours I was superimposing the image of my favourite species over different areas of river, trying to find the place that would offer up the reality. All afternoon I searched up- and downstream, hoping my instincts would tell me where the perch had gone. I concentrated on near-bank eddies or the quiet water behind sunken trees and the inside of bends, but though such places had been productive before – sometimes after wet weather – nothing I tried today brought me anything with stripes on it.

I found a lovely-looking pool between two lines of overhanging blackthorn where the current slowed because of an abrupt increase in depth. I trotted the float down several times and it dipped and curtsied, but wouldn't dive right down. I wondered if I'd found a shoal of roach that were either too small or too picksome to snatch a large worm. As the sun was already deep in the west, I resigned myself to another perchless day and transformed myself into a roach angler. Tying up lighter tackle with a more sensitive float and baiting with a pinch of breadflake, I quickly began to make an impression. The float zipped under after sailing only a few yards and I reeled in a sapphire-sided fish of about half a pound. Then I hooked and lost two in quick succession, one of which was substantial, and suddenly I became completely focused on the fishing.

By letting go of one idea, one dream, and adopting another, the evening took on a different kind of lustre. I lost count of the number of roach I landed, and though many were small enough to swing in, several needed the net and the best one was a superb, deep-bodied specimen of (precisely) one pound and six ounces. But I think what I appreciated most was the slow, easy rhythm of the cast, the drifting float, the retrieve, the re-cast – a rhythm that became more intense yet more mesmeric as the float began to fade into the twilight.

So, although my reel – a Carter Dragonfly – made more music today than it did on my previous two visits, none of its songs contained the word 'perch'. Yet I'm not disappointed.

TWENTY-FIRST
CAST

*When
the
River Is
Right*

My old friend Demus is, like me, getting slightly disillusioned by barbel fishing. We first met, half a lifetime ago, on the banks of our favourite barbel river, and over the seasons we shared many good days. During the last few years, however, the fish have not only become less numerous, but the atmosphere along certain stretches of the river has changed. There is a new breed of angler appearing on the banks, and it seems that modern barbel fishing is going down the same industrialized road as carp fishing, with multiple rods, mass baiting, fixed leads, self-hooking rigs and constant angling pressure on any formerly productive areas.

217

Demus' antidote to this has been his new love of trout fishing, but now it's winter, the trout are spawning, and I said that, if we weren't going to try for barbel, he should come with me to the perch river.

'When did you last catch a two-pound perch?' I asked.

'I only ever caught one,' he replied, 'and that must've been thirty-five years ago.'

'If we go when the river is right,' I said, 'I promise you'll catch another.'

I made that promise three weeks ago and today the river was right.

When we got to the waterside I was happy to see the stream running at a normal late-season level, with just a slight tinge of colour and something promising about its expression. The weather, after a period of heavy frosts, was mild; the sky was overcast and there was an occasional cross-stream breeze. We walked down to the Standard Pool, a broad, gently flowing glide where the depth normally runs from about eight feet at the head to six at the willow-shaded tail.

As soon as we began to fish, the sight of our two floats – two bright-coloured points in a mass of leaden-coloured ripples – took me back instantly to an early morning at my village pond: fishing with a good friend, two red-topped floats vying with each other, the prospect of perch! What other association could I have had?

Demus missed a couple of bites. He fished his float down the midstream line while I fished mine under the near bank. After about twenty minutes, just as I glanced up at a low-flying heron, I heard a thin splash and, looking down, saw a little swirl that I thought was a fish jumping. But it was Demus' float cutting the surface as he connected with his first perch. A frisky, colourful fish came into the net, but it was only about a pound. However, we were satisfied; we'd made a start. Minutes later he got another the same size. Then another. And I hadn't even had a bite. Finally, just after he'd caught his fourth, my float bobbed and I got my first of the day.

We were obviously into a shoal of young perch, because by lunchtime we'd had a dozen and none was much larger than a pound, so we changed pools and went to fish a gap in the avenue of willows upstream. Straightaway we began catching pounders again at the rate of one every ten minutes or so. Finally, I hooked a tiny fish, no more than five inches, and at the same moment Demus hooked something much larger. It ran deep and slow, but didn't do anything dangerous, nor did it demand much line. However, the curve in Demus' cane made me nervous because I thought he was holding the fish too firmly and was convinced the hook was going to slip. The perch turned once from the net, rolling out of reach and looking very impressive just under the surface. Demus gently persuaded it back; it wallowed over the mesh and I lifted it out. We both exclaimed at its size after all the previous fish.

'I reckon you've kept your promise,' said Demus. 'That must be a good two-pounder.'

Picking it gently out of the net and lifting it up, I said: 'I think it might be three.'

It was a wonderfully deep-bodied, broad-shouldered specimen, but the olive green of the flanks was so dark that the black bands seemed indistinct. It was, of course, ludicrous that the fish actually seemed even bigger once we'd weighed it and seen the balance read three pounds and one ounce. After all, if a fish looks big then it is big; we shouldn't have been so eager to reduce or, rather, to expand it to a number. But weighing it also made my promise seem happily hollow.

'You lied to me!' said Demus, as he lovingly slipped his best-ever perch back into its home.

Thinking the smaller fish might have been shouldered aside by their elders and betters, we decided not to celebrate immediately with a cup of tea, but cast again – and were proved wrong. Obviously all the perch in the river, big and small, were in a hunting mood, but as the former are always less numerous than the latter we didn't get any more aristocrats from the willows. It was, all the same, marvellous to watch a float sail downstream, knowing it was going to dart under at any second – and when it did, no one could say, until the line tightened, what size of fish it was. Eventually, though, the swim quietened and the floats remained buoyant. We had our tea, and despite Demus wanting to go back and try the Standard Pool again, I said we should head upstream to fish the Brook Pool, where, just occasionally, perch would gather if the conditions were right.

As before, we introduced no groundbait, not even

a couple of free worms; we just cast gently in, Demus at the pool's head while I fished the tail. Instantly, both floats slid under and two rods began a display of synchronized bending that almost descended into knitting as my fish dashed upstream and the other one headed down. We managed to land them more or less simultaneously in the same net – a parcelling of perch. They were both about a pound and a half – bigger-than-average juniors.

Casting again, I had a dragging sort of bite that resulted in a fine willow branch; and when, next try, the float slowly dragged under again, I thought for a second I was suffering from someone else's tree surgery. I just raised the rod, tightening into something solid and unmoving. But then it moved.

'I think this is a better one,' I said.

The fish steamed ponderously upstream, feeling totally different from all the quick tug-tugging of the previous fish. It lunged out a few yards cross-current and, when the reel sang and I tried to lower its tone, Demus urged me to ease off a bit.

'You don't want to break your line,' he said.

It came in a few yards and the float emerged, hung

a few moments above the surface, then vanished again as the fish made a powerful dive. The reel gave out a long screech that couldn't be silenced until the fish had reached mid-river.

'Can that be a perch?' said Demus.

I had the horrible feeling that maybe it had been a perch, which had now been swept off its fins by a marauding pike. I eased it gradually back and we both craned forward, trying to see what was on the end of the line. As it turned and dived once more I thought I saw a silver flank.

'I think it might be a chub!' I said.

It surged off upstream, and then began to rise to the surface just beyond a bed of dead reeds.

'Stripes!' we shouted.

It was such a happy relief to see the familiar insignia. I tried to steer it round a raft of flotsam, but it wallowed and wove itself down between the floating stems. Demus leaned forward with the net; I kept the pressure as constant as I dared, thinking the hook was going to detach any moment. There was a plunging splash and the fish was out in the open again, swinging round and sliding over the rim of the net.

'What a perch!' said Demus.

It looked a definite three-pounder, but though it was slightly longer than Demus' fish, brighter, with bolder markings, it only weighed an ounce heavier. As I held it a moment in the current, watching its fins readjust to their proper element, the heron swooped over my head again, but I told him this fish was too big – and too beautiful – for him.

It didn't matter that, despite fishing on enthusiastically for a further hour, we didn't get another bite. At dusk we headed back downstream, leaving the river to the heron.

'Is there a reasonable pub round here somewhere,' asked Demus, 'with real ale and a real log fire?'

TWENTY-SECOND
CAST

*The
River
in
Winter*

As most anglers understand, there is something almost religious about the images associated with winter perch fishing: the dull gold of the dead reed beds contrasting with the brightly painted float, the black depths of the eddy under the bare trees, the frosty halo round the low sun, the amazing colours and markings of the fish itself as it rises, flaring and bristling over the net. There are times, however, when I've cursed this seasonal fantasy. Such is the power of its appeal that I've often been tempted out early into some freezing, foggy or sleety morning only to suffer its painful, finger-numbing reality. Today was typical.

After months of low water there has been rain over the last week and the river has at last risen to what, in former times, was known as 'normal winter level'. This morning the valley was greyed by mist and frost. Classic conditions, I thought, for the perch, and as soon as the school bus had trundled off I was out on my joke vegetable patch, digging for bait. I collected just enough to last me till the bus came home again and within the hour I was fishing.

For the first half of the morning I was happy simply watching my float drift serenely downriver. All that mattered was that I was on the river again, absorbed by its subdued beauty. By lunchtime, however, with the sky darkening and a thin wind rising, the float's behaviour seemed monotonous and the river's beauty was turning into a frown. I needed an answer to my prayers, yet it should have been obvious to me hours earlier that there were no responsive fish in my swim. I reeled in, shouldered my creel, and headed upstream to find a proper perch hole.

The weather changed again, even before I'd decided on a new swim, its expression changing from un-friendly to murderous. There'd been no breeze at all when I made my first cast, but by early afternoon a head-pincering gale was sweeping out of the north-east, making laughable all my attempts at float control. For once I wanted the school bus to come home early, but then realized I didn't need to feel guilty about getting back before it.

Now here I am by my woodstove, my life restored to me by a pot of tea. The horde, bless them, won't be here for another hour, so there'll be time for another pot and a reflection on the comic nature of the angler who sets forth in the morning with high hopes and comes home again feeling silly because he didn't pay attention to the weather forecast. It's such a routine event it's hardly worth discussing, but what's interesting is that, though anglers are rarely surprised by a totally grim day, we nearly always maintain our optimism. We understand pessimism because our dreams are sometimes dented by the blows of fate, but always our hope returns, like a primrose after a hard winter. It takes nothing more than the dream fish to glide out of the memory and once again the angler is lifted out of his comfortable chair and into the realms of magical possibilities. It was the same for our prehistoric ancestors. They'd return from a futile day's hunting and slump down in their cave, wondering why they hadn't gone round to the local supermarket. But then they'd see the wonderfully painted images of deer and buffalo glowing in the firelight on the cave wall – and by next morning they were sharpening their spears again.

TWENTY-THIRD CAST

*The
Song of
the Last
Day*

B ecause I can be very patient at the beginning of a fishing day, when I'm just staring at the river, waiting to see if it has something to tell me, but very impatient when I start to fish, I like to keep my angling days as orderless as possible. There's no certainty I'll get any replies once I start asking questions with my line, but if there are no answers in the pools down-stream, then I want quickly, and without fuss, to go and ask again upstream.

The art of angling, as opposed to the mechanics of angling, simply involves observation, appreciation and improvisation; everything else follows behind. But because the unknown element of chance plays such a large part in my fishing, I have to give it as much space as possible in order to take advantage of it. Therefore, I like to have the freedom to roam and follow a whim, which also means that I prefer to be antisocial and either fish on my own or with one, like-minded, semi-solitary friend.

To share the occasional day with a party of companions is, however, always a joyful experience, and every so often, members of the Golden Sale Club – a fraternity of benign fundamentalists – like to gather somewhere on a river to drink tea and sometimes catch fish.

Last year, Jason, who is obliged to run a fairly tight ship, allowed me to take two guests onto his river for the final day of the season. This year, for the same occasion, he foolishly said I could bring five, adding that he'd be joining us, along with another of his angling friends. Therefore, if conditions were at all favourable, somebody's reel was bound to sing. It being a special event in the club's calendar, we agreed to try and reach the river before lunch. Demus and Max arrived at my house for elevenses and it was midday before we arrived on the bank. We thought the others would be waiting for us, but they were already fishing. Somehow, Jason had found them, looking lost, and he'd taken them straight down to the waterside. Besides Demus, no one in the club had ever even seen this stretch of river before; they were all suitably spellbound. The Professor was down under the trees in one of my favourite perch swims, looking like a man in a dream. Jason and his friend were fishing just round the next bend and Angelus was rubbing his hands over a pool downstream.

'And I've brought a cake!' he said.

The weather seemed so perfect after a week of bitter easterlies and the water had cleared so nicely after the earlier cold rain that I said we might not have time to eat it. But someone was missing. The club vintner, Skeff, had originally planned to join us, but Angelus said he'd phoned to say he'd probably be late. Apparently, Skeff had a sudden impulse to fish a different river, having heard a tale about a monster pike. We put this aberration down to the effects of some childhood trauma and, leaving Angelus to fish for chub, we went on downstream.

Demus and I were hoping to end the season with a perch, but Max was more interested in the roach fishing, saying he hadn't caught a river roach for years. I pointed out a likely spot for him, down below a cow bridge, where the river narrowed and deepened, enclosed on either side by lines of old willows. We left him looking like a man who'd just entered paradise and went over to a classic perch hole known locally as the Pier, where there was room for two floats to circle each other in a slow underbank eddy.

In perfect harmony with the surroundings, every-one was using old but elegant cane rods and, mostly, vintage reels, though mine had only been made ten years ago. Demus and I had not long cast out when Max came striding up the bank with what looked like a medium-sized chub in his net.

'Second cast!' he said. 'On a pinch of breadflake.'

He lowered it into the grass, where I realized it was a superb roach – a two-pounder – the best I'd seen on the river all season. Before we released it, I took a photograph of fish and angler together, and as we watched the lovely creature swim away, Demus called to say he'd hooked a perch. However, when it rose to the surface, it was revealed as another roach, quite a good one, though not quite a two-pounder.

For maybe an hour, as the sun gradually faded into hazy cloud, I watched my orange-tipped quill trying to find its way out of the eddy. It was so mesmerizing I couldn't understand what was happening when it dithered and began to move against the flow. What did it think it was doing? Then I refocused, upped the rod and hooked a fish. It was a perch, too; I felt a sharp jagging that suddenly became a dive into the downstream reed bed and before the fish vanished between the stems I saw the stripes. I brought the rod tip over it and carefully worked it free, steering it out into open water. With a final flourish of blood-red fins, it came over the net and I had my last-day perch. However, a few minutes after releasing it, just as I was saying how we might be blessed with a shoal of them, there was a tremendous lunging swirl that sent ripples wheeling from bank to bank and left a vortex that continued spinning for over a minute. Some giant flesh-eater was on the prowl and it killed the fishing at the Pier. Where was a pike angler when you needed one? Why was Skeff so seduced by some old monster myth when he could have come with us and created a new one?

Before we went off to try somewhere else downstream, we agreed it was definitely time to light the Kelly Kettle. I set it up by a big reed bed, next to where Max was fishing, and the dry, brittle stems made a perfect fuel. Within moments a plume of thin blue smoke was rising over the willows and within four minutes the water was boiling. Angelus spotted the signal from upstream, which was just as well, as he, of course, had the cake. Prof was too engrossed in his fishing to notice, though Jason picked up the scent of reed smoke and came to join us.

The tea would have tasted good anyway, but the company, the cake and the occasion made it exceptional. As I prepared a second boiling, we compared experiences. Jason, just back from an exhausting three-day trip to Ireland, had found a very comfortable willow to lean back against, but he'd dreamt of some magnificent fish. Angelus hadn't landed any chub, but he'd had some roach and had hooked a huge perch which broke his line amongst a submerged tree. Max had continued to take fish from his swim – roach, chub and dace – but he said what he wanted now was a gudgeon. He shouldn't have mentioned the magic word because, after tea, I went down and fished a gap in the willows and caught a gudgeon first cast. It was the only one of the day. Max got his revenge by sneaking back to the Pier when the pike wasn't looking, and landing another perch.

I fished my way down the avenue, catching some frisky dace and wondrously coloured roach, but no more perch – not that it mattered. It was enough simply to be in the river's presence at such a moment.

There is something quietly uplifting about a soft grey March day that follows a period of hard, wintry weather. Although the reeds are still withered and bleached, the willow buds will just be starting to swell and the sense of spring is repeatedly carried on the air as a thrush or blackbird or chaffinch breaks into song. I hadn't heard a blackbird since last July, but there was one in the willow opposite me and his voice was low and subdued yet full of promise.

Everyone netted a few more fish, but at around 6.30 we began to lose sight of our floats. I was convinced that a big chub or two would emerge from under the raft of flotsam beneath the blackbird's willow, so I took my float from the line, quickly added a few more shot and tied on a larger hook. Baiting with a fluffy chunk of bread, I cast out and was rewarded with an instant response – from a roach. I cast again, and felt the tackle swing in the current and roll down under the willow. I heard voices: the others were coming to look for me.

'Come on!' called Max, as he found me skulking behind a tree stump. Demus and Angelus came up behind him. 'We've got to find Prof,' he said. 'And Skeff will soon be waiting for us in the pub.'

'This is my last cast of the season,' I said. 'He won't have to wait long.'

They groaned, knowing I was probably lying.

'We don't want to wait, either,' they said.

But they didn't have to wait at all. After a few moments the whole rod heaved over and I struck into something that bulldozed through sunken willow branches and left me reeling air. There was no sympathy from the gallery, just cheers and chortling, but I suppose it couldn't have been a more decisive final moment.

Collecting our bags, rods and baskets, we went in search of our lost comrade, calling his name as we trudged upstream, but there was no reply from the darkness. Had a pike pulled him in? Had he just fallen in? We found him, eventually, drinking tea in Jason's kitchen, looking very pleased with himself. As Jason put the kettle on again, Prof waxed on about all the lovely-looking chub he'd caught, and about the otter that surfaced, slightly disconcertingly, in his swim at dusk. He also confessed to a moment of despair as the biggest perch he'd ever seen slipped the hook just inches from his net.

Jason's boys looked slightly bewildered at having their kitchen invaded by so many loud and large strangers; however, they seemed happy to let us empty their biscuit tin and tell us some of their own fishing stories. Eventually, we thanked Jason for letting us fish his river, said farewell till next season and went off up the road to meet Skeff.

Entering the warm, crowded, dimly lit bar, we discovered him sitting at a table on his own, nursing his beer and looking easily the happiest person in the pub.

'It must be good beer,' we said.

'I've only just got here,' he said.

It appeared his day had been almost as eventful as ours, although he'd only caught seven double-figure pike to twenty-two pounds. By the time he'd told us all about them and we'd retold our stories to him, and compared the day to other memorable Last Days, it was midnight and the close season had begun. When we met again, the river would have undergone a green transformation and we'd have a whole new season ahead of us. But, driving home, it wasn't the fishing, or the colours of the perch, or the swirl of the pike that I remembered, it was the blackbird, because his song echoed strangely in my head and set me thinking about seasons in a slightly different light. While we, as a race, change our tune every generation, the blackbird perfected his long before there was anyone to hear it, and now all he needs to do, once every year, from March to July, is sing. His beautiful voice has been ringing through countless springtimes and is now one of those reassuring constants that can draw me deeper into my chosen reality. The river's voice is quieter, more mysterious, but just as essential.